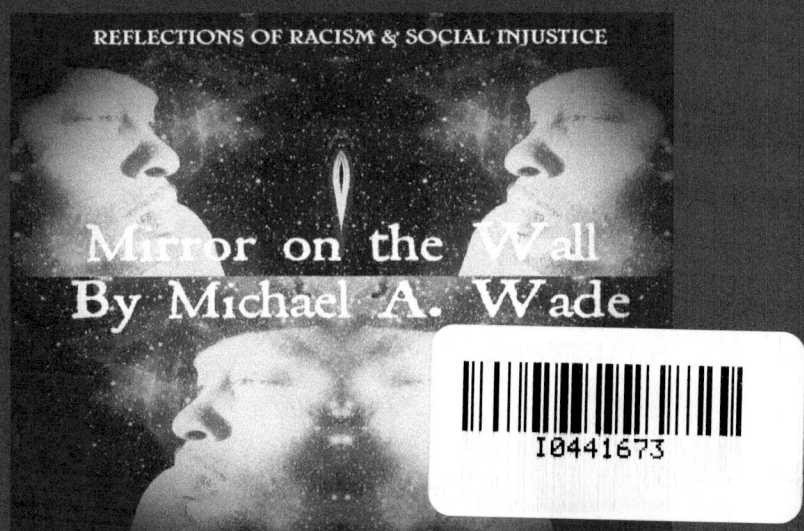

REFLECTIONS OF RACISM & SOCIAL INJUSTICE

Mirror on the Wall
By Michael A. Wade

I0441673

POETRY& ESSAYS TO STIMULATE THE SOCIAL CONSCIOUS

I've come in touch with the evils that are embedded into the DNA of my soul.
Now that I have removed myself from its allure I find my own darkness scares me more than my fellow man himself. Why call it evil, it is more of a primitive, raw emotion manifesting chaos. For in this too we find it to be a part of the human condition. –Michael Wade

Mizchief's Ink Publications 2016

TABLE OF CONTENTS

PUBLISHER NOTE

What you are about to read are short essays and poetry based on the current subjects on the social conditions here in America. These writings dwell deep into matters of raw, unfiltered truths and unresolved issues that exist among us as Americans here in the United States of America. Racism, class-warfare, stereotypes; the deliberate miseducation of the people; these ills plagues our as humanity and handicap us as a people. As the citizens believe the politicians will solve these issues for the people; only to watch the flames rise and communities' crumble around us.

There will be those who claim this book will add to the division among the American people or the world. They will say the author is perpetuating hate, and trolling. THIS WILL NOT BE THE TRUTH. Let's be clear on the authors' intentions. This author abhors racism or bigotry of **any type** or in **any combination of races**. The author feels we're humans first (the most advanced species) and Americans second, (the most advanced society on this planet,) we have access to enough history to where we can see the destruction careless division causes. Yet we tend to try to solve problems by asking the wrong questions.

The authors' and publishers' purpose for this book is to help educate & stimulate the thought process to begin asking the right questions. Bring unity and common understanding among first to the human race, and more importantly us as the citizens of the United States of America. White Americans needs no longer to fear being traitors amongst their race, as Black Americans no longer need fear being called Uncle Toms for being able to get along with Whites in American society. BUT make no mistakes; the author is speaking out against the plague of White Supremacy and its ideology that brings the various

2

racial and economic divisions in America; implemented policies which cause the disparities which are acknowledged by politicians and the powers that be. Ranging from, the United States Government down to our local community councils.

By reading this book you will be forced to look at the ugliness within yourselves and your own contributions to this social condition. Does White America does have an obligation to help right the wrongs their American forefathers put on the Black Community? Do Black American Communities have a lack of accountability? Do the negative actions and thought processes that added to the devastation excuse the behaviors, thoughts & actions produced? Willie Lynch taught White American Slave Owners how to capitalize on shaping mindsets of Africans, and he was successful.

The Human Race is not made up of two dimensional creatures; there will always be different perspectives as well as views on how to solve problems. This book is written with the purpose of stimulating the thought process towards building bridges and creating solutions, and we will never be able to come up with solutions if first, we continue living in the problem. Passing the blame onto each other by choosing to remain ignorant to laws (past & current) purposely created to oppress people. To merely say you know racism, class war-fare and the miseducation of a people exist and do nothing to affect its change is not enough. Three, stop the perpetuation of a systematic dismantling of a people historically known to be suppressed.

The author/publisher does not speak for the Black Community or any other Minority Communities, and in no way would attempt to be so arrogant as to do so; he is just an observer... a watcher. The author educates and displays a fresh perspective, with a genuine care and concern for the people and the issues that affect us all. So keep an open mind as you take a current look at the reflections of racism and social injustice as we gaze into the "Mirror on the Wall."

-Mizchief's Ink Publications

THE DAY THE ANGELS FELL FROM THE SKY

I saw it; it was the day the Angels fell from the sky.
The day no one knew what or why.
Can anyone tell me what happens when Angels fall out the sky?
Does anyone know what this will mean?
How much hope will this wither away?
What will live or die?
Will this mean I may never fly?
Does this mean no more Heaven & hope dies?
Being raised by cold hearts prepared me for this day.
Singed white feathers fall to the ground like snow.
This phenomenon has me questioning all that I know.
What happens when Angels fall out the sky?
I saw the silhouettes in the lightning flashes imprinted clearly.
Each flashes a picture of Angels falling out of the dark, bleak &
dreary heaven.
Raining the fall of glory, a storm of immortal death,
Michael, Gabriel, Arch Angel after Arch Angel.
One by one the Angels were falling out the sky in numbers like
raindrops.
Thunderous thuds as these heavenly beings & the earth came
face to face.
This day the hearts of men became heavy,
For to whom will they turn to?
Who will be the appointed guardians of the souls of man?
Who will God put in charge?
…Where is God?
As the tears fall down peoples cheeks;
Dampened dreams,

Did this mean there would be no tomorrow?
This was the day the Angels fell out the sky.
No God to answer what, how or why.
Can anyone answer what happens after the Angels fall out the
sky?

"THEIR AIM WAS TO TRANSFORM THE NEGROES, NOT TO DEVELOP THEM. THE FREEDMEN WHO WERE TO BE ENLIGHTENED WERE GIVEN LITTLE THOUGHT, FOR THE BEST FRIENDS OF THE RACE, ILL-TAUGHT THEMSELVES, FOLLOWED THE TRADITIONAL CURRICULA OF THE TIMES WHICH DID NOT TAKE THE NEGRO INTO CONSIDERATION EXCEPT TO CONDEMN OR PITY HIM."

-Carter Godwin Woodson (1933), "The Mis-Education of the Negro."

I AM A BLACK AMERICAN

I am a Black American with no African ties, so why am I called
"African American?"
Born and raised on new world American soil.
White Americans aren't referred to as Euro-American.
Aren't their descendants just as foreign to this land as mine?
Does it not take more than a dark complexion to say I am
African?
Last I checked, in Africa, there are pale, white humans with
British accents calling themselves African.
Judging from my American history I have no ties to those people
either.
My African ancestry cut all ties the day of the great new world
kidnap caper.
Africa extinguished family-ties the day it sold their sons and
daughters for a meager price.
Never has Africa asked for, or fought for the return of Black
Americans any time in history.
Hundreds of thousands made it to the new world, as millions lay
dead at the bottom of the sea.
I AM a Black American.

The audacity of those who label me African-American!
This is not to disrespect the black brothers & sisters from Africa.
But I will not live a lie. Who does the name African-American
disrespect?
It disrespects those Black Americans who have fought & stood
for me.
Revolutionary War, Civil War, Spanish War, World Wars, Cold
War, Vietnam War, Iraq War.

The label belittles the blood spilled from family members beaten
& torn from me.
In the name of building a "Great Nation"
Do not the red, white & blue speak my Black American story?
Red represents the blood of those Black Americans whom were
beaten & killed in the name of America.
White, for the hoods and robes blacks would fear, also represents
the dominant society who is in control.
Blue, for the sea where millions of black bodies lay at the bottom
and the sky Blacks look at to dream.
The Stars, for the night sky Blacks would look at to help guide
their escape to freedom.
I AM a Black American.

Blood has been diluted generations over with Native American
blood and blood of the slave master.
So what other than complexion makes me "African?"
Is the dark-skinned Cuban any less Cuban because of their
complexion?
Or a Brit from Britain that is descendent from slaves any less
British?
I think not!
No need to be reminded of the "Great Oppressor" or of the
injustice or inequalities Black Americans face.
Black Americans know our plight.
The word "Nigger" is not exclusive to the United States.
Other countries may use a different name or word; it does not
make the meaning any different.
If I was to go to any African country, they would hear me speak
and would say, "You're American."
I AM a Black American.

My spirit descends from Fredrick Douglass, Medgar Evers,
Malcom X, and Martin Luther King Jr.,

From the Great Black-American spirits that refused to die.
White America may want to but cannot deny the Black
American contribution to building this nation.
How is the black contribution denied? Just check your history
books, what do you not see?
Check the Constitution & laws created throughout history.
The wilderness Black Americans were once lost in is now
familiar and is their home.
YES I AM, A PROUD BLACK AMERICAN!

DEEP IN THE HOLE

As I stood over this deep shallow hole, pondering over its depths
Feeling weary, spirit weighted down, eyes locked onto its
darkness.
This shallow, dark hole held a whirlpool of visions.
I saw life's accomplishments, disappointments & regrets
These things are the ingredients that make man & woman
human.
The deeper I look the more I recognized my reflections of good
& evil
A chess game; pieces moved by the fingertips of fate & destiny.
This hole holds a purpose of finality
Trails of memories that begin to a path of a future unknown
With the same ending promised to us all
Time waits for no man
But the deep hole waits for us all.

"NOT ALL WHITE AMERICANS ARE WHITE SUPREMACISTS, BUT ALL WHITE AMERICANS DO BENEFIT FROM THE PRIVILEGE THAT WHITE SUPREMACY PROVIDES, HAS PROVIDED AND CONTINUES TO PROVIDE. A PRIVILEGE THAT IS WRITTEN & UNSPOKEN, KNOWN & HELD DEARLY TO HEART."

-Michael A. Wade

"IMITATION BECOMES A FIXED HABIT. NATURALLY THE CHILD IMITATES, FIRST OF ALL, ITS PARENTS! THEN IT BEGINS TO IMITATE ITS OTHER RELATIVES AND DAILY ASSOCIATES, INCLUDING ITS RELIGIOUS INSTRUCTORS AND SCHOOLTEACHERS."

-Napoleon Hill, from the book, "Outwitting the Devil" (1938)

POISON PIE (A LETTER TO THE BLACK YOUTH)

Dear Black Youth,

No, you do not know me, but today I come to you first as a Black man, a father, a son and then a brother. I speak from a place of concern for your existence as well as your future. I am not only addressing the black youth, but the poor Whites, Hispanic, Polynesian and Muslim brothers and sisters, for you too are afflicted with the symptoms of these plagues in this country called America.

I am not here condemning or persecuting your ways in which your generation chooses to live. But you should understand! The status-quo has you labeled as "thugs, savages, militants, terrorist, criminals, gangsters;" some of these names you wear as badges of honor. While once you're in the system you find names on paperwork referring to you as, "assailants, attackers, defendants, offenders, convicts, delinquents, felons." Words used to demean your value in society. Words used in the propaganda which all media uses to make your community fear you... It is working! **Wake up**; I and others believe in you, so I am asking you to collectively use your ways/recognize your purpose, your power, use it to help bring about a better equality.

The line in the sand has been drawn in a room void of light. In fact I am here to turn the light on that darkness. For I too once shared the destructive mind-set of money, hoes & clothes, a mind-set the media exploits and chooses to **flatter** you with. By appealing to your inner most desires; taking the desire to express yourself and using it against you; killing your aspirations, replacing it with fame and money. In many cases you are cursed

14

with fame spreading no further than your local neighborhood streets; being compensated by the nickel & dimes that are picked up off city streets. This evil is not only handed to you directly from your enemy, but your family & friends whom bought into the lies from your enemy about the glory of crooks. **The negative conditioning of your minds**, this negative conditioning is plaguing the minds of the minority youth beginning at an early age. Jails and prisons are not homes to rehabilitation or reform. They are the breeding grounds to a new slave-class of people, the **"Felony Class."** A class of people (mostly young minorities) with felony convictions on their records, so 15 to 20 years later after paying dues for crimes & building legit track records, **society will remain condemning** the felony offender.

This will mostly affect the non-violent offender since it is safe to assume and can be supported by national statistics that our prison system is mostly made up of non-violent offenders. This will be done by the legal act of denying inclusion of Constitutional of Rights and then by not recognizing you as human under the Human Rights Act.

Due to your new label society will use this to define your place in the community. Allowing community leaders and businesses to set social & business policies that deny inclusion back into mainstream society and the opportunity for your pursuit of happiness in the community you live. Even when it is clear a positive moral change has occurred. I am not here to preach, but to warn you about life after the hustle, to help you prepare yourself. For that reason I feel it is my duty...No, my obligation to reach out to you.

My generation, your father's generation has failed you. Just as your father's father generation had failed him. I will go one step further to say, those who attempted to stay or fill in as surrogates have failed and misled you. By showing you a way of life that is **developed & designed** to keep you on the track of this **"felony class."** On track by not protecting you and educating you to these dangers; not informing you (black & white races in particular) of past history and policies used and created and redesigned for today for the oppression and control the people. Lack of instruction in the preparations of avoiding these crucial vices of, selling drugs, living by the gun, spending your money foolishly (a.k.a. financial discipline), disrespecting, stereo-typing and down-grading of women in our society.

These actions delude you into exhibiting a lack of **self-control,** while leaving you thinking "you are in control," supporting the belief these actions are qualities that make a man a man or a woman a woman. Watched by our government and recorded in the system to be continuously used against you, securing you as a new millennia slave in the status-quo, counteracting your quest to a better quality of life. Prison numbers don't lie and cannot only be seen statistically, but in the bank accounts of businesses involved in the building of The Prison Industrial Complex.

There is a term coined for a species in the wild that has become unable to recognize the enemy, Naïve Prey Syndrome. This term can be applied to you. The time to educate your-self and wake up is now!! These aren't just mere poisons, but **glorified poisons** presented to you as sweet wines; offered in unequal exchanges. Poisons placed at your tables of living, **disguised as desserts**. These poisons are not new; for these are the same traps that were presented to your father's in their youth are now presented to you. It was named "**The Big lie**." "The Big Lie" has now been **repackaged, remarketed, redistributed** for your destruction today. The players have changed, but the game remains the same.

The sad truth is all of you won't make it. Some have to die so others can live. There will always be good and evil in any form fathomable. You can no longer afford feeding them the bullets (the reason) to deny you an existence, by turning your dreams to a living nightmare; replacing them with false hopes. Turning your necessities second to your wants; investing your God-given talents into a proven falling stock, the set-up for a slow timely suicide for riches of no substantial value. Not meant to better your life but worsen its condition, as if its current condition is not already in need of repair.

Being **"hood rich"** is not a trophy, it is saying your hard earned money is dirty & will never live up to the elites. The elite say their money creates generations of wealth, while the poor and middle-class create rich moments. Those in power who exercise this ideology and brandish its power dictate the best place to hide information on the reaching of success is to put it in a book; think about it.

The information you are presented is a false vision of reality, the system needs you to believe in this false vision of reality it creates. Local and national politicians acting as systematic Gods; mortal prophets who profit from the spoils of the degradation of their own humanity along with those they influence. These false-prophets claim to share your struggle, as they speak of them-selves as intellectually greater; **why aren't they uplifting you? Why aren't they educating, creating opportunity, while being the leaders they claim to be?** Instead they sell-out and the cycle perpetuates.

Singing & dancing is supposed to be a time to get together, forget our problems, rejoice & celebrate. I don't know if you've noticed, but the system has you singing, dancing, and celebrating the very problems you are running from, getting high and committing crimes to forget. Are you paying attention?????

This letter is for the youth, from the age of understanding my words to 25 years of age, I am talking to you. (Not excluding anyone older whom which this shoe fits.)

When the neighbor has been taken out the hood was when the Black Communities began treating each other like cold strangers. No longer trusting neighbors; reducing heartfelt communities to straight dwellings. Now the community's young people are being seen as a danger.

Thugs & gangsters; mission accomplished you have pumped fear into the hearts of all humanity. With all your tattoos, sagging skinny jeans, sparkling jewels, dark mystique, and macho bravado; you have manage to strengthen the dark cloud of the minority stereo-type. Perpetuating the belief those cursed with poverty are nothing but animals that eat their young.

But hey, it's all in the "game," right? Has history taught you nothing? Haven't you been paying attention? You are being fed rope to hang yourself in efforts to justify a systematic injustice of the lower class. In the age of information & G.P.S. most of you are still using out dated maps to success. It is time to evolve, if these communities are actually your hoods than take care of them along with its people, take some real ownership. Your block shouldn't fear you, they should respect you. Old folks shouldn't have to worry, they should feel protected. Yes you have some responsibility for the ingredients in this poison pie as well. We understand you did not create this market you service, but doesn't mean you can't take control of it. For if you are a product of society many of you claim to be, then you have responsibility to the ingredients in which adds to its condition

Re-organize & re-focus; here is your opportunity to **prove the world wrong**. Show the people you are not the savages they group you with. How about helping flush out these children sex offenders, or don't some of you have kids that play outside? Maybe redirecting the fear you instill in the communities into the clientele you serve who terrorize civilians in the name of your product. Let the parks be free zones for the babies to play. Hmmm, what a start huh?

Knowledge is power and with great power comes greater responsibility, I'll say it again, with great power comes greater responsibility. **Don't let yourselves be led by men who vision a future with no humanity!!** The cost are young brothers like,

Trayvon Martins, Jordan Davis's, Jonathan Ferrell's paying with their lives, their deaths being products of the fears you've helped pump into the veins of society. You have shown them prisons made up of concrete & steel will not hold you. This fear has them now killing the innocent.

Prison numbers equal dollar numbers & numbers don't lie!! 1 in 3 young black males in America can expect to go to prison in his lifetime, numbers turn to 1 in 6 from the ages of 25-54 for black adults. In the **plan for Black American/minority unification** (a plan so generations may flourish is in the works.) We will account for you, have a place for you and the talents you waste in turmoil, but will not count on you or protect you as long as you keep feeding the monster which divides the people.

Dear Government, this does not relieve you of your responsibility for the support of & implementation of the **malicious rules & policies** put in place that **supports irresponsible governing, miseducation and oppression of the people. The people will no longer wait for those high off ignorance to wake up to join the revolution.**

But today I talk to my young brothers and sisters, for we cannot **focus on the solution** of the systematical machine until we address solutions towards our own self-induced inflictions. We must stop feeding our enemies the bullets to the proverbial and real guns aimed at your head. Stop repeating the failures of history, those were lessons not meant to be forgotten. You don't have to shoot or be shot to know if you pull a trigger something or someone may get hurt; or even die!
It is time to step up there is too much below you for you not to be on solid ground. Recognize, do not repeat mistakes made, so you may be that much closer to success. Continue to **break the mental binds** that Willie Lynch helped cultivate in the Black Community. I say that to say we cannot

continue to discredit, disrespect the accomplishments & advancements of generations prior. The first tactic in the Willie Lynch manual was to put separation between the young & the old. No longer, we need our history, we need the truth! Now is the time for young & old to stop the bickering; get your heads in the game; just **as the struggle updates** we must too **update our approach in attacking** it.

To the Civil Rights generation, respect these **young, intelligent, remarkable game-changing** young men & women; they are not the turn the other cheek type of generation. There is too much history that supports those types of based practices does not work in the protection of a people. Non-violence does not stop people who mean you harm. Wrong is wrong and there are corrections that need to be made, this young generation knows the truth and will no longer accept being lied to, or fed fairy-tale stories and accept it as history.

Time is now, **focus economic & political powers**, no community is taken seriously when voicing change if it does not have the ability to self-sustain, and that's economics 101. Also depending on how much real estate the community occupies will determine the political importance of those people on the political spectrum. Young brothers and sisters, recognize you will never financially strengthen a community by only striving to be drug dealers, rappers, or sports stars. Those are not the only avenues to financial independence; although glamorous those are not the careers that will sustain a community.

Well plotted distractions have you all falling for the same political tricks over and over. It is not too late; time is our only enemy when it is unproductive & uncultivated. So I say wake up young people the time is now, wake up, the time-is-now.

"I HAVE A FOOL PROOF METHOD FOR CONTROLLING YOUR BLACK SLAVES; I GUARANTEE EVERY ONE OF YOU THAT IF INSTALLED CORRECTLY, IT WILL CONTROL THE SLAVES FOR AT LEAST 300 YEARS."

-Willie Lynch (1712,) "The Willie Lynch Letters & The Making of a Slave"

DADDY WHY?

CHILD ASKS:
Daddy why do you have to work today?
DADDY ANSWERS:
So I can provide for you the things you need.
To show you what a good man can be
In hopes that when you grow you'll be a better human than me
I wish work wouldn't take up our time together
I work so hard to see you smile
I work so you may enjoy being a child
Its work that takes me away from your sporting games,
award ceremonies, amongst other things.
I don't have what is called P.T.O.
That is what employers call "Paid Time Off"
So for me to support means it will cost
Income lost
Mean mugs from my boss
More over time,
Work harder to catch up
It's a vicious cycle that won't let up
They say because I'm not at home
I am a deadbeat, while you're free running wild
They call you a gang-banger; I say that's my child
So as I work, I pray your playful actions won't send you to jail
Even more, I worry about what you wear may get you killed
I'm not absent from the home, I'm at work
I only get to see you every other weekend
Mother doesn't understand until child support comes up short
I have to work today so that I don't end up in court

Or in jail cause I can't keep up with the current along with the
back dues
So I don't lose more work along with a confiscated driver's
license too
So this is why I have to work 10-16 hrs. a day, 50-80 hours a
week
Working for a below cost wage to keep feeding 2 ends that will
never meet
The system lures fathers away from the home
Keep robbing Peter to pay Paul
They figure if I'm not home that you can be better parented
through laws
With this in mind I live for the moments I get to spend with you
Although those moments seem so few
Watching television will have you believe
That Daddy abandoned you, making daddy appear like a jerk.
Daddy loves you and I want to play, but I have to work.

THE MULFORD ACT OF 1967:

THIS ACT EFFECTIVELY RESTRICTED CITIZENS FROM CARRYING GUNS IN PUBLIC AND CREATED ONE OF THE COUNTRY'S MOST STRICT GUN CONTROL REGULATIONS. THIS WAS A DIRECT REACTION TO THE BLACK PANTHERS.

RIGHTS VS. CONTROL

Why do people believe they can change a countries nature with no repercussions? The United States of America was founded with the belief of the people's right to bear arms. Let us tell the truth & shame the devil. Guns were used to make this country what it is today; from the time the English & Spanish settlers came to claim this land. Even when they crossed back over the water to retrieve slaves; guns were used.

America's Founding Fathers knew after dealing with the English (a government armed with an arsenal.) That the ultimate way to stay protected was to keep firearms of our own. Let us ask ourselves, would the English government have taken the people of the New World seriously without the people being armed? ...I think not. With that being said, the enemy that means you harm will not take you seriously knowing you have no means of protection equal or greater to theirs.

When it comes to Assault Weapons, they are just that; **ASSAULT WEAPONS!** Built for assault & harm, if you hunt with them they destroy what you're hunting. If used for home protection, you yourself will end up destroying what it is you are trying to protect (at the minimum destroying your residence.) Now brings the question, should the American people have access to this type of weaponry?

YES, as great as America is, we all can agree our government cannot be trusted to do what is best for the people. "Power corrupts" words spoken by one of this very country's founders. That is the very reason the people were given the right to bear arms for, to protect themselves from a government gone awry. "...A well-regulated Militia, being necessary to security of a free state, the right of the people to keep and bear arms **SHALL NOT BE INFRINGED**." How can we defend ourselves if the potential enemy has access to greater fire power?

With that said, we have become a country who tries to control so much of the people's actions that we have negated personal responsibility. It is sad, heartbreaking, repulsive, and maddening to think about what happened in Newtown, CT. Nothing feels worse than to outlive your children (yes I know.) But the answer to this situation is not putting armed guards at the schools nor is it banning weapons. **THE FIRST ASSAULT WEAPONS BAN DID NOT WORK!** Ask the "Cocaine Cowboys, Iran Contra and the gangs that toted AK-47's in the 80's and 90's.

Unfortunately the young shooter had no business having access to any type of arsenal, he was mentally unstable, and the mother (the responsible gun-owner) knew it. Now should that crap on her 2nd amendment rights...? NO, but when a person chooses to have a mentally unstable person in a residence that carry guns than the bar is extremely raised and punishment severe for failing to reach it.

Why not, as we can see, the alternative is stomach wrenching. The issue has become how to keep guns from the mentally disturbed and the criminals; instead we make laws to hold guns back from those who are not criminals.

Hold accountable the owners of these guns when they fall into the wrong hands. Cut off the licenses of these gun shops/sellers that do not due their due diligence. YES, ALL **GUN SELLERS HAVE A RESPONSIBILTY** TO MAKE SURE THAT THEY ARE PUTTING GUNS IN RESPONSIBLE HANDS. It is owed to the community they serve JUST AS MUCH AS IT is the peoples job to **KEEP GUN'S OUT OF OUR CHILDREN'S HANDS,** and keep them safe.

People need to stop using criminals as the excuse for gun control! They sound like idiots! Convicted criminals are not purchasing fire arms from mainstream gun retail stores. The majority of the people committing these heinous crimes are people without criminal records, think about it. 2007 Virginia Tech college shooting, 2009 Fort Hood, 2012 Colorado theater shooting, 2012 Newtown, CT school shootings, 2015 San Bernardino, Orlando 2016 were all committed by people with no criminal history. So if this is the case why are our law makers focusing on those already fully restricted to handle guns. There are laws already in place to handle the felon in possession of fire arms.

Guns aren't the problem; access to guns is not the problem. Is it any better if a person uses a blade; a sharp instrument to kill, or a hammer, a pencil, a pen? It is the mental conditioning aligned with circumstance that makes a killer; not the tool a killer uses.

The people have been conditioned to believe that a part of obtaining true "justice" is having the offender of said "justice" to be made an example of. In example, the mass shooter; the people want to see the shooter punished or made example of so in hopes that anyone else who thinks to attempts such horrid acts repents in fear of the consequence. There is one problem...What is to happen when all you have left is an ugly act with no one to punish? When the killer gets killed or commits suicide, who is there left to make an example of? How do we bring closure to such tragedies? Local and Federal Governments seem to believe those burdens fall on the shoulders of the people they govern.

Through social and government policies they show that their belief is that the breakdown is in the private sector; the citizens.

Are we willing to turn our schools into prison fortresses for our children to learn in? With all the talk going around, we will have imprisoned ourselves if we aren't careful.

"NO NEGRO WHETHER SLAVE OR FREE COULD EVER BE CONSIDERED A CITIZEN OF THE UNITED STATES..."

-Roger B. Taney, Chief Justice, U.S. Supreme Court1640

PUSH THE TARE BUTTON!

Precedence has now been set in the New Millennia America people. The justice system has now made it okay for the police to murder black families, armed or not; without the officers being held accountable. This reaffirms the Black Communities distrust in police officers who chose, "To Protect and Serve", a motto so overly used. This has affected the black community since the creation of America, and will continue to affect the black community if the tare button is not pushed. To the white community make no mistakes this will affect you as well; for if policemen and women are going to kill blacks with no gun, who are only perceived as a danger, not a real threat; all the work Black Americans and White Americans have put into closing the racial divide will be lost. Whether it is looking suspicious in a hooded sweatshirt while walking home, selling single cigarettes on the street for a quarter or walking in the street, OUR society is in danger. A good enough reason to come to the table (Black Americans and White Americans) and make right the wrongs so true equality can reign. How can we do that you ask?

First we need to understand police history and the foundation on which it was created; by White Men in the name of White Supremacy. Countless acts pertaining to the Black Community shows this, as White American history supports this statement.

Originally known as the "Watch" system, started in Boston, Massachusetts in 1636; New York followed suit in 1658, Philadelphia, Pennsylvania in 1700. These "Watchers" were made up of volunteers from the community whose only job was to warn of impending dangers. These men ("Watchers") were known to take the job to evade military service; they were drunks and sleepers on the job. Even worse some were forced to do "Watch" duties as a form of punishment by the community. In Southern states the police was known as "Slave Patrols" created in the Carolina colonies in 1704. The "Slave Patrol" had *Three primary directives: (1) chase down, apprehend, and return to their owners, runaway slaves; (2) to provide a form of organized terror to deter slave revolts; (3) to maintain a form of discipline for slaves who were subject to summary justice, outside of the law if plantation rules were violated.*

Starting in the 1830's American Police Forces developed a local, centralize bureaucratic police force. After the Civil War this vigilante-styles, often corrupt police forces evolved into emerging respondents to disorder, violence against immigrants and Black Americans by the white youth was the top crime of its day. They were restructured in the name of economic interest for social control rather than crime control, used as enforcers for the laws and policies that governed the land. Slave codes with a make-over; the Jim Crow laws of the 1880's; the Black Disenfranchisement Laws of the 1900's; the systematical laws and policies created after WWI that purposely affects Black America and the poor white and minority communities to this day.

New structure calls for *Three new primary directives* given by the commercial elites: *(1) to insure a stable and orderly work force; (2) a stable orderly environment in which to conduct business; (3) and the maintaining of the "collective good."* Once again enforcers of laws and policies that protect an economic interest, an economic plan built on the oppression of the black race. Similar to the guard dog; simply expected to guard persons or property and often to attack or restrain on command. But has anyone thought to stop to ask, who watches the guard dog?

We can look back through the 1900's and directly correlate police conduct in terms of their mentality when it comes to the Black Community. They have been the over-seers, punishers, judges and in many cases executioners. Many blacks knew of police men who were pro-Klu Klux Klan, if not members of the terroristic group itself. It wasn't till 1911 America had its first Black American Police Officer, Samuel J. Battle.

Now even more currently in the 2000 millennia we have states implementing policies like NYPD's "Stop N Frisk." Where in the Park Slope community of Brooklyn 2011, where Blacks and Latinos make up 24% of the population, they constituted 79% of all stop and frisks. Guns found in less than 0.2% of all stops, while 88% are not found guilty of any crime. There is also Federal Law 287g that allows the stopping and questioning of immigrants and their status without probable cause. Laws mirroring slave code laws of past times are still holding true today. It is said that law enforcement officers are trained not to believe in coincidences...well neither do I.

The "Slave Patrol" mentality is still deeply imbedded into the psyche of law enforcement and the policies it enforces. We don't have to go back to Jim Crow times to find examples of this racist mentality in justice. 1991- Rodney King; 2002- Donovan Jackson; 2009- Oscar Grant III; 2014- Eric Garner, Dontre Hamilton, Tamir Rice; 2015- Walter Scott, Freddie Gray;2016- Alston Sterling; 2016-Philando Castile. Many feel that the 2014 Michael Brown incident was the exposing of police brutality in Ferguson, which in this authors opinion was not the case. The Michael Brown incident was the exposing of the racist/oppressive systematical tactics communities across the United States are using against Black & minority communities across the nation. Using police forces as income generators to fund their oppressive policies; very reminiscent to Constable times of the early colonies.

Now that 27% of minorities make up America's police departments and the same mentality has made a cross-over. So much that we can talk about cases like Kelly Thomas, a mentally ill white man who died at the hands of police brutality. Black Officers have found themselves perpetuating the same police brutalities on young men in Black communities. While upstanding Black Officers have become victims of police racism inside and outside departments; making it harder for the good officers to do their jobs. We may never truly get to see good police if good police never root out the bad seeds amongst themselves. The same ones who swore an oath to protect the community are constantly involved in the killing of it. How are we to thrive as a people if we continue to constantly take attempts at assassinating human evolution? The people feel the badges power have deafened the ears of those under oath to protect our American cities. Law & order has mistaken the peoples distaste for the endless brutal policing in neighborhoods as a lack of admiration.

Only by reviewing the law books & examining the social policies specifically made for the oppression of the black and minority communities will we balance out the scales of justice. There is enough history in the "information age" to know the nature of these laws and policies created and for whom they were created. Once found these unjust laws and policies need to be stricken from the legal books. If necessary the ousting of any politician or city board member whose actions supports the same old way of doing business. Those in power need to feel the power of the people as a reminder that they serve the public not the other way around.

After laws and policies have been destroyed and reconstructed a restructuring of law enforcement procedures needs to take place. There is a major disconnect between the police and the communities they serve. A connection that has never fully been a positive one for the Black Community; most officers who patrol the black communities today do not come from or live in those communities. Policemen ought come from or live in the communities they serve; personal investment is crucial in the protecting of a community/neighborhood. They have to interact and connect with the people; bring death to the mentality that police are dealing with animals in the Black Community. The more people relate to one another the less race even becomes an issue, because you have other information to process when dealing with people. The Black Community is not asking to be handled with special treatment or with kid gloves; they are asking for a respect from the police that historically has never been given to the Black Community. Asking not to be racially profiled in their own communities has become too much to ask for. For a White Police Officer to go to a black neighborhood and say, "We're looking for a black male, 5'9, in jeans and a sweat shirt who was looking suspicious." Is the same as a Black Police Officer going into a white community saying, "We're looking for a white male, blonde hair, blue eyes, 5'9, wearing work boots, jeans and a t-shirt."

Accountability! The lack of accountability of holding law enforcement accountable for its notorious conduct throughout history is sickening. The countless numbers of black lives knowingly loss due to police brutalities will never be forgotten. Not until 2015 does Black Americans see a police officer being arrested and held to the fire for killing of a black man. Accountability is a must if law enforcement will have any connection with the Black Community. The hundred plus years of brutality against the Black Community by police departments across America will not be forgotten. The countless number of senseless murders of Black Americans committed by the police; victims who will never have justice.

Police Officers must police themselves and hold each other to the highest standards in order to be blameless when question of integrity arise. Along with a community over-sight committee strictly focused on police relations in the community; a separate entity from the city council that controls the handling of city policy. This committee will have to be able to assure the community that accountability and transparency are remaining a constant.

Let us not fool ourselves any longer into thinking the scales of justice are balanced. Bring death to the ideology of blacks who do wrong are whining of getting no justice... No! Zero that out, The United States Government cannot amend constitutions, give equal civil rights, and keep the same oppressive mentality in its policies and say the system is just. What happened to the betterment of the "Collective Good?" Black America is now and has been a vital part of this "collective.

There are people of the law in the United States, both black and white, i.e. Presidents, Congressman, Legislators, Governors, Democrats, Republicans, Judges, Prosecutors, Defense Attorneys, and most importantly those who teach law all agree the justice system is broken. If you're not going to listen to those who are affected listen to the people who create the laws and policies. Same politician who sat and watched as a nation suffers from the madness these policies help create. By not attempting to solve these issue supports and contributes to the continued inequality that governs the U.S. today. It will not be enough for black activist groups to picket police stations without attempting to affect the legislation which controls and governs the land. Protests are only good in conjunction with affecting the legislators who bring the rules to govern. It's like trying to sue the guard dog for biting you and not the owner themselves.

Sources: *Eastern Kentucky Universities School of Justice Studies/ Police Studies*

Bleausa.org , "Modern Police Policies Rooted in Old South Slave Codes," article 6/10/2014

Newsweek, "The New Racial Make-up of U.S. Police Departments," article 5/14/15

"I HAVE NO PURPOSE TO INTRODUCE POLITICAL AND SOCIAL EQUALITY BETWEEN WHITE AND BLACK RACES. THERE IS A PHYSICAL DIFFERENCE BETWEEN THE WHITE AND THE BLACK RACES WHICH IN MY JUDGMENT, WILL PROBABLY FOREVER FORBID THEIR LIVING TOGETHER UPON THE FOOTING OF PERFECT EQUALITY, INASMUCH AS IT BECOMES A NECESSITY THAT THERE MUST BE A DIFFERENCE, I AS WELL AS JUDGE DOUGLAS, AM IN FAVOR OF THE RACE TO WHICH I BELONG HAVING THE SUPERIOR POSITION."

-Abraham Lincoln, 16th President of the United States of America

Source: Brainy Quote.com

TOGETHER WE STAND, DIVIDED WE FALL.

As a Black Man it seems at times Black Americans cannot win for losing! Five hundred plus years at the bottom of the world's pecking order. Black Americans, we are (what seems to be anyhow) the most hated race in the world; mostly hating on each other.

There isn't another minority race in America that is more scrutinized than the Black American. A race demonized by its justice system while their systemic problems are sensationalized in the media. Presented as moral-less whiners to the world; Black America stays systematically oppressed as the world watches the oppression exploited on the Hollywood big screens and television. Part of the problem is Blacks and Hispanics are being treated as second class citizens in their own country. Although (historically speaking) the Hispanic/Latino Community has received preferential consideration in civil matters over Black Americans when statistically and historically speaking.

I admit we Black Americans don't make it any better. Black Americans will act as if nobody cares about or sees anything that Black Americans do. Be aware Black America, Black Americans are always being watched even while they sleep. Black Americans are a danger to their enemies especially when Black Americans dream. Black Americans actions are watched and recorded on everything they accept as a community; i.e. the broken slang they call "Ebonics" as if Black

Americans don't have the ability to sound educated. White America calls it "Talking Black." Toleration and excusing of a criminal mentality, a way of life; due to Black America being shut out of economic opportunity. We will stand in line for a pair of $200 shoes; spending a week's worth of pay. But won't spend money in the Black community where we live, support talented Black artist and business men. Some Black Americans will even game the system at our own expense; welfare, child support, the return policy at your local stores. Making rich moments from ill-gotten gains; not investing in your own communities much less yourselves. I've heard so many Black brothers and sisters in my time say, "Go to the county/state office get that money, that's what it's there for." Or my favorite, "The government owes us!" Which depending on whom you talk to of color may or may not be true. But the reality is…

THE UNITED STATES OF AMERICA IS NOT GIVING BLACK AMERICANS ANYTHING!!! This was made clear by **General William Sherman** and **President Andrew Johnson** in **1866** when he **vetoed the congressional bill** that would have gave Black Americans **40 acres and a mule**. Yes that cut us deep, so deep that some Black Americans carry that chip on their shoulders till this day.
Blacks Americans have long memories; genealogy does not forget.

2016, America has never been "post-racial," who in the hell invented that term?! What happened was after the Civil Rights Movement of the 60's, which was (let's make no mistakes) the death of Evers, Shabazz, King, and the dismantling of the Black Panthers; it became the burying of racial equality issues for Black America. The United States Governments racist, murderous actions swept under the rug the remaining equality issues Black America fought and died for. Robbing Black

America of its hope and unity; causing Black America to settle into its current condition.

Now Black Americans today stay divided willingly! I say that because there is not a Black American who isn't aware of the Willie Lynch tactics. There is not a Black American who is not conscious of how White American slave owners put Black America in a mental slavery that has outlasted their physical slavery. Breaking the string of dependence on one another was the only way the White Slave Owners could keep their control. Keep Black America as its subservient class of people. Mission accomplished, it has and is working.

No more does Black America have to be subservient; no more does Black America have to be victims of our past. Black America's ancestors in Tulsa, Oklahoma have shown us that by creating Black Wall Street. Black America can thrive in a White Supremacist country without White America. No I am not saying we should go back to segregation, but the reality in this country and the world is that each community must be self-sufficient or risk being society's underclass which Black Americans currently are. Do we not see this with the Jews, Chinese and Hispanic cultures in America? This does not mean the different cultures have to be at each other's throat. This doesn't mean the different cultures cannot work together to make this country what it was destined to be.

White America what can I say, but you've been lied to. White American Millennials the lies have been passed down to you as you have been included into the miseducation of society; for the sole purpose of perpetuating the White Supremacist agenda. I believe the term the Government uses is "Plausible Deniability." This "Plausible Deniability" has a large portion of

White America in a state of denial even when the facts are clearly shown.

History teaches us that yes before the 15th Century Whites were once slaves too. But as Americans we have come to believe slavery to look like what Black Americans went through. That was not the case for White Europeans; White European slavery was known to be mutual agreements. A way to pay off debt, there were term limits to their servitude and the beatings as punishment was unheard of. Also during their time in slavery once their servitude limit was up bonus compensation was often given for the completion of their servitude.

How did this change you ask? Have you ever heard of the "Mameluke Rebellion of the 14th Century?" The Mamelukes were Arabs attempting to establish world power; owners of the last group of "White Slaves." These white slaves believed the only way to get the freedom or equality they wished for was to revolt; forcefully and vengefully. It became one of the world's bloodiest, most gruesome rebellions known to man. It was so horrible that it ended the general enslavement of whites by the Arabs forever.

The Europeans of the 15th Century were well aware of this history (the 15th Century mind you is when Black African enslavement by Europeans began.) This knowledge of the Mameluke Rebellion was passed all the way down to the early colonist who became the Forefathers of the land we call America today. This became the reason American Colonist/Forefathers feared rebellions from the Blacks for this very reason; which is why the American enslavement of Blacks was nothing like the world had ever known. Strict laws were made by White Settlers/Americans forbidding the teaching of Blacks anything outside of slave labor. Although labor was taught to slaves by other slaves.

The original American economic plans foundation for the building of wealth in this country was built on the use of Blacks as its slave/subservient class. An economic plan built by White Europeans and adopted than carried out by the White Supremacist Forefathers. A plan that history shows has not been changed but added to; I believe the government uses the word "Amended."

White America wake up! Nothing changes if nothing changes. The time is now to make this the United States of America what it was destined to be; **<u>UNITED</u>**! What the American Forefathers have done was inhumane and reprehensible. The same shameful ideology was passed down to the grandsons and granddaughters of these Forefathers, the White Supremacist power structure who continued these oppressions. Unfortunately your ancestors left you, todays White America, holding the bag. Now what are you going to do about it?

We hear all the time in each political season about, "What will we leave for the next generation?" It is clear what White American Forefathers left for their next generations; it is documented in diaries and doctrines of people who are known as "Great Men." These lessons are taught in schools to children by teachers with books designed to teach anti-black standards. Now made into a nation-wide curriculum where teachers are punished for diverting from it; misleading and misguiding their own children the offspring of these Forefathers in hopes to continue what once was; that their white privilege stays intact.

Now it's 2016, we live in the information age where information is King. Where there is a large fraction of White Americans waking up seeing and learning the lies on which "White Privilege" was built. There are many White Americans that have become disgusted with the truth of their ancestral history and disgusted with Whites who are in power that promote this division and do nothing about this systemic problem. White Americans see that equality is not being equally distributed among all Americans. But unless White Americans in large numbers stand up against White Supremacy nothing will change; until White America sees their "White Privilege" is at the cost of non-white Americans nothing changes. Here is another hard truth; the White Supremacist powers that still have a hold on this nation cannot afford for everyone to be on one accord; all cultures, all races. Yes, in 2016 the White Supremacist power structure is still alive and present; so much it attempts to make a comeback in the 2016 Presidential Election.

With the sweeping of race issues under the rug after the Civil Rights Movement, Americans have been herded like sheep into their perspective communities in society. Giving the illusion that Americans live in a "post-racial" society; all because America has integrated the different cultures within its populations. But if you look closely Americans can see the division by which policies & laws are applied according to the different communities. You'll be able to see the division by how the different American cultures are directed to live in certain areas of cities across America. And just when Americans thinks we are healing racially someone picks the scab and Americas unresolved issues of racism and social injustice shows its ugly head in situations like; Trayvon Martin, James Byrd, and James Craig Anderson. *THIS CYCLE HAS TO STOP!*

Make no mistakes, as Americans (Black & White) we have made progress; there are places in America when race pops up as an issue the said problem gets dismantled quickly. There are communities that have risen above the racial dynamic and see human problems as human problems. The media won't show you these places. Hollywood depicts these places as imaginary;

as something to aspire to. There are people who wish not to believe these communities exist; there are people who would have you believe that this sort of harmony between Blacks and Whites in America does not occur. Unfortunately these are people who would paint a picture that humanity is forever lost; and it will be if Americans keep letting destructive politics and corporate greed destroy the people's unity. People have been so abused systemically that they cannot see the forest through the tress. Let's be clear, when acts of racism and social injustice happens anywhere in America it is a threat to everyone in America.

Have we not lost enough loved ones over this senseless, shameless division over race? Are we not now all Americans? **MESSAGE TO ALL AMERICANS:** Remember "separation" was a major tool in Willie Lynch's tool box, so take note; also tactics in each version of the Art of War. So it would be safe to believe that the powers that be (government and private entities) are using the same tactics against their own people; Black Americans and White Americans.

Today our separation gap has gotten so deep that we left room for the enemy to come between us as Americans. Disturbing any if not all the progress we've made together as a people; by letting our civility reign over emotion. Using today's most powerful tool as a divisional tactic, Social Media; hiding and instigating. Playing both sides against the middle causing us to put at risk any progress we have made; no matter how small or big. We have people taking us out, as we fight amongst each other. The outsiders are only able to do this only because we (the people) have not solved these race issues between ourselves. Not that I have anything against any other country, but America is my home; and I'd be damned if I let anyone come in my house and take advantage of my family's problem for their own gains.

There you have it news media, Mr. President, so-called black leaders and any other person or representative that I have heard on television saying that, "We need to start the discussion on race." Or "When are we going to talk about the pink elephant in the room." The last discussion was mighty bloody and ended with the assassinations of many of our own Black Americans; along with the killing of White Americans who stood along with them. Nothing got resolved, issues got buried, and what could not fit underground is now falling out of the closet. And I could be mistaken but White America is in shock learning of all of the lies as Black America is no longer willing to turn anymore cheeks, every time we do it seems we get smacked in one cheek turn and kicked in the other. I'm just saying I could be wrong. So the next time you hear Mr. President or anyone for that matter say we need to start this discussion on race let him know the dialogue has already started and they are late to the conversation, because I've been sitting at the table and none of those people have shown.

A KING WITHOUT A KINGDOM
(The Black Man's Journey Home)

I was a man, a father, husband, provider... I was King.
You were on my side a woman, a mother, wife, nurturer, ... My
Queen.
There was nothing I could not accomplish without you.
I built you pyramids & monuments to withstand time.
I was yours & you were mine
The world & its knowledge was ours to wield
The finest garments & jewels
Bathed you in the finest natural oils & sweet perfumes
I loved the way the sun light enhanced your beauty
Ruled lands farther than the eye could see
Then out of nowhere a curse fell upon you & me
The day became dark, but the darkest we have yet to see them
The day I became a King without a Kingdom

Strange white men kidnapping the women & kids
Killing the elderly, enslaving the able young boys & men
All I remember of that day was the screams & loud booms
Yelling from these pale men calling my Queen & daughters
wenches
Before I could get to you they beat me down and hog tied me to
a stick
I recognize the pale men's helpers from over in the next village
In & out of consciousness I saw you chained to others in a line
Distraught crying in agony with tears in your eyes
It was your fear that gave me courage
For I broke those binds
I was coming to save you from this crime

I then felt a pain I can't describe
Woke up chained to others taking a bumpy ride,
I immediately called out to you
To find you in my voices reach
You relay to me how the situation looked bleak
You were scared
At the bottom of this dark vessel laid & bound to strangers
Positioned in fecal matter mines & theirs
My Queen yells, "Please no sir, I'm soon to be a mother!"
The diseased are dying before my eyes
All I could think is how to save my Queen & unborn child from
demise
Passed back out, dreaming of being with them
As I laid, a King without a Kingdom.

Dropped & gathered on this New World shore
Not knowing what was in store
I found you & held you tight
Promised everything will be alright
I lied.
At that moment you & our unborn was snatched
These enslavers lit my rage so in my rage I fought back
They were about to kill me
You begged for them to spare my life
You cried & pleaded for me to stop the fight
You whispered one day we'd be together
Then everything will be set right
So because of your plea
I stopped fighting
Watched you be sold & carried away the same night.
The memory of your last words gave me hope.
Hope that one day you'd be back by my side.
I will see that day, I will stay alive.
A King without a Kingdom

I was sent to different fields to work
Daily threatened with death by whip or rope
Word came back to me where you stayed
You had our child & was only a few miles away
On my first only attempt I found your window
To find the Master having his way
You saw me & mouthed, "Please go away"
I refused, this wasn't right
So I busted through the window to go after the Masters life
You put yourself in harm's way
Told me to run & you'd always love me
I vowed to come back
I struggled to run in the dawn of day
Only to be caught & marked as a runaway slave
Tied me up & whipped the flesh off my back
As you stood & watched holding our son
They made me an example in front of everyone
Beat me within an inch of my life
For being a beast running wild in the night
For being a Nigger going after a White Man's life
With each lashing visions vanishing of a land called home
My screams came out loud as roars
I showed you strength
While tears filled my eyes, & pain in my heart
You said, "*Find your way back to me*
Give up your fight stay alive."
You'd be lost to me forever,
The evils my mind could not fathom that you've endured
I failed to protect you
A chinked armor, broke the man inside,
Forever my disgrace, a black-eye to my pride.
On that night, for you I should have died.
A King without a Kingdom.

I worked the fields for Massa; all day with no pay
Did what "Massa" say do
Staying alive so I may one day come home to you
Put me against other slaves in nightly death matches too
Rewarded me with females & cold suds
He called me his finest stud
The females were for breeding
He said I made the finest pups money could buy
Making kids for the slave pipeline
Keeps me locked & chained over night
When Massa looks into my eyes he says something isn't right
To run became only a thought
Freedom a fairy-tale, an unknown paradise
Although my want to come home to you was always there
I held fast till opportunity presented itself
A King without a Kingdom

The Missy threatens to yell rape if I refuse her advances
She calls to me when "Massa" goes drinking with other
"Massa's"
She fantasizes, makes me do the things Massa don't
It would be best if one of the field bosses would walk in
Shoot me on the spot
Keep from hanging, torches burning hot
Luck has never been on my side
So I endure
What a wretched curse; where is the cure?
In time I lost myself
A King without a Kingdom

I traveled through time
With Massa's ideology ruling my mind
Moses came for me but I was blind
Then the soldiers arrived
I joined the war that made a divided country wider in its divide
In hopes to have a freedom promised
In hopes I'd be able to make my way back to you.
So I fought doing all I had to
Then one day it was over & I was free
Free to travel as far as the eye could see
You was nowhere in sight
I witnessed the horror against other women wondering if you survived
In my heart I knew you were alive
I will find you in time
A King without a Kingdom

I searched for you, my Queen
Remembering what you said
Find your way back to me
So that's what I did
You had been through so much
You said our son grew & embodied his father's spirit
The white man killed him because he feared it
This tribulation has our souls misaligned
Far from the life we lived once upon a time
I worked the railroads even the mines
We started to argue & fight all the time
Worked hard all day to come home & rule the roost
Started doing all the things Massa taught me to do
Beat my woman & kids when they got out of line
Philander with other women all through the night
Fighting with Black Men who were doing better than I
Liquor & envy drove my anger

As I come to see
Yes, I'm no longer a slave, but I'm still not free
Jim Crow, Red Summer a new danger for you & me
Reconstructing what use to be
A King without a Kingdom

We seem to come together you & I
In a different dynamic, a sign of the times
Immigrants came organized & introduce me to organized crime
For every hundred I make they let me keep a dime
I entertained on the side
Still my love for you never died
To take care of my family King am I
Garvey said Black Nationalism was the answer for you & me
Wrote you poetry, a sweet serenade
We created a Renaissance, seeing the error in my ways
Our Minstrel Shows became the talk of the town
You singing in a hole in wall lounge
Whites mocked by doing shows painted with black face
For the money Minstrels were making they wanted a taste
To deal with my woes I sang Jazz & the Blues
To deal with my anger invented Rock -N- Roll too
Only to find the White Man taking that too
Taking my credits for inventions in medicine & science
Taking my knowledge making themselves financial giants
While Jim Crow wouldn't allow me to cross the tracks
My Queen could crosses to be there maid & that is that
Left our children dinner on the stove fending for self
To nurse white children, to keep them in good health
Before dark you better have your ass back cross those tracks
The sun is setting run & don't look back
A King without a Kingdom

I grew tired, wanted better for us, a positive change
I became civilly committed to help Black people rise again
Our oppressed greatness was seeping out of our family's pores
Society's inequalities of freedom affected us to the core
The death of Emmitt Till, Rosa Parks seat
100 years after slavery they say the 19th amendment was made
for me
The black man's rise to peace, the crowning of a King
Only to have X mark the spot
Of the anger & hatred that was stewing in this melting pot
For Evers, the fight for voting rights could start
You & I together as examples of courage & hope
Bringing our people together, teaching new ways to cope
A King without a Kingdom
Our children became wild cats against social injustice

Celebrated the power among us
The world heard you & I loud & clear
The King & the Queen stood together again
But the slave master changed his name to the status-quo
Stood against the uplifting started destroying all we know
Assassinated the different parts of my soul
Evers for populating voting booths
Shabazz for no longer being the opposition he was made into
Dethroned a King for not turning the other cheek when it came
to back pay
But you still supported me,
Through all this you stayed with
…A King without a Kingdom

It was too good to be true it didn't last
Hoover vacuumed the last hope we had
Destroyed every black cat in its path
With no pride or hope I felt ashamed
I left you alone, I left in vain

Life became too much I couldn't take the pain
Walked away from what we built step by step
Into the new slavery, the prison industrial complex
Help to enslave the mind of our youth
Yes I am guilty of that too
Teaching our boys how to be men I left that to you
How alone you must have felt
What a hand to be dealt
A King without a Kingdom

You were trying to teach our children right
I was back on the plantation being Massa's finest stud
Downgraded my family beliefs
Due to being left out of society financially
Indoctrinated the children into gangster mentality
Gave the kids a new family
I was their Daddy I was Blood, I was Crip
It was I alone who paid for what Reagan, Bush & Contra did
I only made times harder for you
The weight was heavy to relieve your burden I began pimping
you
To handle that burden I fed you drugs too
Left our children to be raised by the status-quo
I became what was expected by the status-quo, unraveling all I
know
A King without a Kingdom

As I laid in that cage images ran through my mind
All you & I been through in time
Everything from the capture to the divide
The beatings, rapes, the constant injustice in our lives
The invisible barriers put between you & I
I have to make right what I've done wrong
Bring back a pride & hope to a family that is all but gone

All of these thoughts had my pilot light re-lit
20th century almost over, all I forgot I had to be reacquainted
I'm going home
A King without a Kingdom

Now that I have been home for some time
Reclaiming the throne that is rightfully mine
Media would have you believing otherwise
Trying to reverse the damage to you & I
All the miseducation, all the lies
Restoration of our family ties
Teaching our children about my mistakes
Teaching our children a history Europeans tried to erase
All our covered up accomplishments
This countries racist historic doctrine
To show America I am a permanent citizen & a resident
To show you the world could be yours I became America's
President
But my struggle continues
Still a lot to fix, a lot to undo
All the misguidance, the misleading of the youth
My worthiness I will prove to you
My Queen I have found you
I have found us…I
A King without a Kingdom

"WHEN A MAN IS DENIED THE RIGHT TO LIVE THE LIFE HE BELIEVES IN, HE HAS NO CHOICE BUT TO BECOME AN OUTLAW."

-Nelson Mandela (1918-2013)

UNEQUAL OPPORTUNITY

One of the biggest overlooked forms of discrimination in this great country in which I live is that of the convicted felon. Even after paying back society for their crimes with prison time, probation, restitution, etc., it has become an acceptable practice for corporate businesses to condemn felons within the communities where felons are released back into; supporting the belief that felons are unredeemable commodities & only have a place doing menial, low wage jobs; even if they obtain or already possess the skills necessary to thrive & be a legit success in Corporate America. Not all businesses mind you, but more than a handful. Leaving the convicted felon struggling to make ends meet for their families, denying them the honest living for which they are qualified for; supplying the same oppressive conditions which helped create this dilemma to begin with. WHY IS THIS AN ACCEPTABLE PRACTICE????

The story you are about to read is true, the situation very real. The company this story speaks of is Comcast/Xfinity a NBC company. The company who has recently attempted to buy Time Warner for $45 billion; giving them control over the majority of the countries cable systems & any other services that they may provide.

After being released from prison in 2002 to parole/probation for non-violent crimes committed in the late 90's. I started my journey to redemption, not an easy road as I have had my bumps & scrapes along the way, but expected societies push back & no matter how frustrated I got, I knew I would have to pay my dues. Prove to society that I was worth redemption & that I could develop/operate with a moral code that was aligned within the rules/laws of the community to assure peace.

In June of 2007 I finished paying what I had owed to society for my past transgressions. By this time had held many jobs. Working mostly two-three jobs at one time, collecting necessary experience; building a resume that prior to my conviction was non-existent. Working mostly office jobs, collecting accolades from bosses & employees who knew my past & were proud of the person I was becoming. I held a determination to succeed even though my work experience was me sitting at a desk; I even impressed the bosses when employed in manual labor positions, a work ethic those good ole boys respected that.

Nevertheless, my criminal bill was paid & I knew if I wanted to continue down my road to success I would have to leave my home state where I had friends & children whom I love/adore & who love/ adore me back. So I moved away to start new beginnings & leave my troubled past behind me.

It didn't take me long to find a job once I got where I was going, plus it was a job doing something that I loved to do, working at a world renowned gym as a membership director. I held the job for a couple of years before they ran into financial trouble & went under. I was not discouraged; I was no stranger to hard honest work by this point, in no time I found temporary employment at a fast food restaurant mopping floors, cleaning grease pits & toilets. During this time I took my memoirs/poems that I wrote while in prison, cultivated & self-published my first book an autobiography, "My Power, My Pleasure, My Pain, My Life in Poetry." In which I had my first taste of publication success. During my time at the fast food restaurant I knew that the job wasn't a permanent place where I intended to keep employment so I kept searching for 8 months only to successfully find a job with the nation's leading bank Wells Fargo. Here I would get a rough lesson in office politics as I never experienced before. A taste of Corporate America's entry level, here I would stay for a year not liking how the company operated under the guise of customer service (where all my experienced lied.) As well as promoting team work while management supported the development of in-house clicks & encouraged the stepping on those in lower positions to climb the "corporate ladder." I knew I could not sustain employment in this type of environment, so I remember what my father told me when I was a teenager, "If you don't like the way things are done here go get your own." So that is what I did and started Mizchief's Ink Publications. I would stay with Wells Fargo Bank for another 8 months afterwards before we would part ways while working on self-publishing my second title working on my third.

I held part-time employment while developing my company in its infancy until those part-time jobs went away and Mizchief's Ink became a full time job. For 3 years I sustained financially with book sales, promoting at open mic's & book fairs. Counseling other writers/authors in the art of self-publishing, I learned more in those 3 years than I ever could have being an employee at any other job in that time. The woes/successes of operating a business, the true value of teamwork (seeming I was a one man operation in the publication business), plus the discipline & determination it took to operate. It gave me a new found respect for those who employ.

Now it is 2014, things became steady with my company to where I WANTED employment so I can have medical benefits and still be able to work my company part-time (I was not giving up on my new found dream.) So I as I went to Comcast/Xfinity to pay my cable/internet bill also to disconnect my cable & internet (realized it wasn't worth the money for what they were offering), I noticed the sign saying they were hiring so I went on-line and applied. Within a couple of weeks I received a call. After talking to the lady who was a part of a staffing agency the company used to hire new recruits, she was impressed! Stated,

"You are exactly what Comcast is looking for."

So she e-mailed me the links to take the personality assessments, told me that this is a "requirement" and if my score was high enough that she would be able to move further with the hiring process. So 24 hours passed after taking the test and she was delighted to move me to the next step, the interview process.

There was nothing personal about this interview, they had rented a conference room in a hotel 30 miles from where I lived to work at an establishment 10 miles from my residence (no problem.) It was a job fair style interview process that ran for 8 hours (10am-4pm.) I got there early one of the first 5 people to show ½ hour early, signed up on the list as the group of applicants got larger. We all waited in the cold hotel lobby excited about the opportunity. They called everyone in to the conference room where tables were set-up with 10+ recruiters sitting and waiting.

I was prepared, the first to sit down with one of the Comcast Recruiters who had also been impressed when I gave a brief description of my background (on how I reinvented myself in the last 3-4 years.) Being impressed he congratulated me then proceeded to ask me a list questions to get a feel on my experience in certain situations. After asking his list of questions he too believed I was what Comcast was looking for, within 72 hours of that day I received a call from the Comcast Recruiters wanting to move on with the hiring process.

I was elated to be chosen to work for a conglomerate like Comcast, so I read up on them & how they were restructuring themselves to be more customer friendly & outgoing also how the company was broadening their horizons by expanding in other entertainment & technology territories. I figured by me being in the publications business this would be the place for me to be.

So a different Comcast Recruiter called me from another state (the main office I imagine.) She informed me that I will be receiving some links to fill out info on for a background check along with the info to set up an appointment for drug screening. She advised me that what they were not concerned if I had a past just as long as the information matched up so do not leave anything out.

So I set up my appointment for the drug screening and filled out the background check information. I gave them 10 years + of personal information including my 15 year old felonies from the late 90's, every address, education, the long list of jobs that I've held including showing them that I have been successfully self-employed for the last 3-4 years.

After going back and forth by e-mail for 2 weeks with the company who conducts background checks for Comcast, requesting information, I get a final e-mail requesting explanation on my criminal background (which I had already given.) So I look at the copy of the info that they pulled up from the criminal database, confused as to why are they asking for an explanation I had already given. I noticed everything matched up but a misdemeanor offense that fell between the two felonies I had failed to disclose. So I gave them the explanation & send back the e-mail.

Valentine's Day, I still haven't heard any word concerning the decision coming from the backgrounds. I have no worries; I had been truthful & forthcoming on my past & had given the requested explanation. Besides it has been 15-16 years since I received any convictions and have a good track record to back me up on turning my life around.

I finally receive a call from the Comcast Recruiter; I had to return her call because I initially missed her 1st call. I call she answers, I then introduce myself, tell her I apologize for missing her call. I could hear her smile over the phone as she assured me that wasn't a problem. I lightly joke saying I was wondering when I was going to hear from Comcast seeming it was Friday and the training class starts on Monday. She apologized and informed me that they just received back my drug screen & everything came back fine. But then there was a pause, she starts out by saying there was a misdemeanor that came up that you did not originally mention. I replied,

"I saw that in the e-mail I received from the background check company & I sent back the explanation as requested."

With hesitation in her voice she said,

"Uh…Yeah concerning that, we will not be able to offer you employment for that oversight."

I replied,

"You're kidding me right, it was 16 years ago. It wasn't as if I was trying to hide a misdemeanor after admitting to the two felonies, one that happened before the misdemeanor & one I committed after."

She says,

"I know, but it is a company policy & we have to treat everyone the same."

So I ask her,

"This cannot seem right to you, it is obvious that I wasn't trying to be dishonest or keep it from you. There has to be something we can do, it seems ridiculous to deny someone a livelihood for forgetting about a misdemeanor after they admit to two felonies one of which occurred before the misdemeanor."

There was a hesitation in her response as if she was thinking of what to say, you can tell my response had resonated with her. She finally spoke,

"This is what I'll do I'll give this to my supervisor and I or her will give you a call back to let you know what we come up."

I reply,

"Thank You, I'll be awaiting your or your supervisors call."

Upset at the decision I wait for an hour and no call so I call back, the Comcast Recruiter herself surprised that I had not received a call back. So she puts me on hold to see what the hold-up is; I'm on hold for like 2 minutes she comes back & says her supervisor will give me a call in an hour. I once again tell her thank you and add the statement,

"I refuse to believe Comcast/Xfinity is so inhumane to deny someone a livelihood over a misdemeanor transgression I forgot about that is 16 years old; after already admitting to things far worse (the 2 felonies.")

We hang up and I wait an hour and a half, still no calls so I call back, I'm patched through to the Recruiter Supervisor. I introduce myself then asked if her employee had filled her in on the situation; she says she has,

"Unfortunately, we are unable to go any further with the hiring process due to the undisclosed misdemeanor."

I ask her,

"This cannot seem just to you? To deny someone a livelihood for a mere evident oversight; what is a person supposed to do keep a list of his life's transgressions?"

She replied,

"Sir, it is not about keeping a list, and just to be quite honest with you we would have denied you employment anyhow for the other crimes you admitted to."

Now the truth came out, so I replied,

"Once again, are you kidding me I admitted to those I was told as long as things matched up, besides all these crimes are over 14-15 years old I paid my dues for these crimes, so what you're telling me is Comcast/Xfinity is going to hold crimes that are 15 years old against me? Comcast believes that once a person makes a mistake no matter how long ago that they are unredeemable?"

She says,

"Not my words sir."

I say,

"Sure those are your words if your only reason for not giving me a position with your company is for transgressions a decade and a half old. The Federal Gov't doesn't hold anything against you past 10 years, come on! They weren't even violent crimes!"

She comes back with,

"Sir, guns are violent."

I say,

"No they're not people are, what you see are possession crimes, you should really do some studying if you're going to make statements like those. My crime is drug and gun POSSESSION crimes! Not assault, not manslaughter or murder! I refuse to believe this company would be so inhumane as to deny a person a livelihood for admitted transgressions in which dues have been paid. I've even worked for Wells Fargo; I can work for a bank but not the cable company? You're treating me as if I am trying to hide something. I have nothing to hide in the last 4 years I self-published 3 books one of which is my autobiography. I became a productive member of society that owns his own business this has to mean something."

She responds,

"Either way sir you failed to disclose the misdemeanor so we cannot go further with your employment, my hands are tied it is company policy."

She continued to bounce back and forth between the felonies and misdemeanor, I responded,

"No they are not; you're at the top of chain the buck stops with you! Instead of hiding behind a company policy that is evidently wrong for this situation, I'm pleading with you to do what is right, help me. Let me prove to your Comcast/Xfinity people with felony convictions can change, I'm asking you to stand with me, do what is right for the situation not hide behind your companies policy. This cannot seem right to you, more than likely just like you I have mouths to feed as well. I do not want to believe that a company can be this cold & dismissive."

She says,

"I'm sorry sir; you're more than welcome to re-apply in 6 months."

I said,

"Are you kidding me!!!!? What changes in 6 months, the same record that you said Comcast/Xfinity will not hire me for anyhow will still exist; the state my crimes were committed in a state which does not expunge criminal records. A state I no longer live in and have not lived in for 6 years."

She replied,

"I'm sorry sir it comes back to the undisclosed misdemeanor."

Being fed up by this point, because evidently I was not getting through to her, she could care less. So I left our conversation with a final statement.

"Thanks for the non-opportunity."

Then I hung up.

If this is not a form of discrimination than what is it? It has become an acceptable form of discrimination. Yes, every man is free except the enlisted servicemen and the convicted felon. The difference is when the enlisted man serves his military time he is considered a freeman once again, but the felon is not even after the debt to society is paid. The felon is forever cursed to be marked as "slave," to be a wanderer in a nation who can only be redeemed in death, forgiven by God.

This is the very contradiction of "All men are created equal." These businesses have no problem taking felon money, matter of fact the day before I received a call from Comcast once again trying to get me to pay for their services. I'm good enough to be a customer but not an employee. It is companies like this that gives business a bad name. Companies that set up shop in communities take monies from all of the community but wants to ration out opportunity. These types of practices says humanity does not exist when it comes to business & employment. We live in a world we're everyone has to be given an equal chance to succeed in employment for those who seek it, otherwise we as a people we are feeding the very issues in which we abhor: homelessness, welfare, Government hand-outs. Road blocking the unalienable right to the pursuit of happiness; which in America having stable employment is part of that pursuit.

Now will I starve because of this, NO, I have my own business and a support system which ensures I will eat another day. But what about the many felons who this has happens to who don't have any other means to eat but to work for someone? Everyone cannot live off hope the stomach does not accept it as sustenance and utility companies do not accept hope as payment. And when you kill the little bit of hope in humanity these felons do have do not be surprise when the crime rate rises. President Obama's "Banning the Box" is not enough! Let us not give our convicted any excuse to return to their criminal ways, there are more felons who want to do right than be stuck in those revolving doors of the justice system. There has to be a cut-off time for transgressions to be legally used against the convicted.

For me this situation has lit a fire in me unlike any other, someone told me long ago, "If you can't find something to live for, than find something to die for." I have just found both.

The struggle continues.

"THE ODDS ARE ALWAYS AGAINST
THE RUNT OF THE LITTER. THEN
WHEN I GO OUT TO COMMIT A
CRIME, THEY SAY, "WHY DON'T YOU
GET A JOB?" CRUCIAL CONFLICT."

-Michael "Mizchief" Wade, from the spoken word piece "I
Can't Change"

<u>DON'T HAVE TIME TO HATE</u>

I don't have time to hate!
There is not enough money in the world that can make me
devote my energy.
Why taint my spirit, bruise my synergy?
Keep digging in the dirt you're going to find something that
doesn't want to be found.
Hate is an evil action an awful sound.
Never matches up with morality.
Hate is a way to act violent without acting violently.
Like death it comes silently.
Hate you for your color?!
Hate you for your race?!
Let me talk to you for 10 minutes.
I'll find 100 better justifications that will bitter your taste.
I'm no punk, I refuse to give in.
Hate is a diseased whore, easy to obtain in this modern day
living.
It's just no damn good!
Hate is the only reason I need to be better.
I know it exists.
All shapes & forms stay hater resistant.
I don't have time to hate!

Too many good things to focus on
Why focus on the evil?
Why take a strong outlook & make it feeble?
I don't have to like you
But I don't have to hate either
I can be indifferent & walk right by you

POOF, once again you're a perfect stranger
One I wish not to know
Because what I do know of you I cannot bare
You hate my success; it is not going anywhere
Let your envy of me be your motivation to do better
Your malice for me keeps your feet planted at the bottom of the
sea
Stagnated, drowning your own success
I'm a trailblazer, a leader, in positivity a creator
I let my known haters be my known motivators
I don't have time to hate.

REMEMBER TO FORGET

Remember the American Revolution
The oppression, over taxation of the New World
Forget Slavery
Remember America's Forefathers
The making of a country, the freedoms of the Constitution
Forget the cocaine user, the Marijuana grower, and slave owners
Forget Black American Slavery
Remember the Industrial Revolution
The birth of financial independence in America
Remember the Civil War
The lives lost; the coming together of a nation
The freedom of a people
Forget Black American Slavery
Remember the Spanish-American War
Remember the Gold Rush, the birth of the Wild West
Forget Jim Crowe; Forget Southern Disenfranchisement Laws
Forget Black American oppression; Forget Black American
Slavery
Remember Theodore Roosevelt, Carnegie Steel; the earthquake
of 1906
Remember the Model-T
Forget the Klu Klux Klan, forget reconstruction
Forget the thousands lynched & killed Black Americans
Forget Black Wall Street, forget the Red Summer
Forget Black American Slavery

Remember WWI the beginning was the end
Remember the death of Carnegie, the rise of Hitler and...
Remember the Hindenburg & the stock market crash

Remember the Nazi's, the Holocaust & the Jews
Remember the Great Depression
Forget 500 years of continued Black oppression
Forget the injustices & assassinations
Forget Slavery
Remember the Cold War
The cold, ruthless dictators
Forget the fight for Civil Rights
Remember Vietnam
Forget the brutality of Police Dogs & the spraying of fire hoses
Remember the plot against the Kennedy's
Forget the government plotting against Shabazz, Hampton &
King
Remember school programs that fed starving children
Forget that it was the Black Panthers who invented it
Forget Huey & Bobby forget the two Black men who facilitated
it
Forget the Black Panthers
Remember Hoover & Reagans dismantling of them
Forget Black Slavery
Forget your history,
Remember to accept your place
Forget white privilege that White Supremacy Provides
This is the United States forget about the racial divide
Remember the empires of America & Rome
Forget it was against the law to read about Egypt & Africa Black
Man's original home
Forget that they stole Blacks history so it may never be known
Remember to forget.

"A KIND OF RACISM STILL EXISTS IN
THE UNITED STATES, AND
ISLAMOPHOBIA IS A MORE
CONVENIENT WAY TO EXPRESS
THAT SENTIMENT. THERE HAS ALSO
BEEN AN ATTEMPT TO PAINT
MUSLIMS AS ENEMIES OF THE UNITED
STATES."

-Feisal Abdul Rauf

Source: Brainy Quote

ALONE AMONGST MANY

The world was content as I stood & screamed silently with a
smile
Some people stopped & stared; in a trance of awe & amaze
With phones on record watched as the gun was being raised
In a crowd of many
I put a gun to my head & pulled the trigger
You might find the film on your Facebook or Twitter
Mine being one in a billion choices you will have to crave your
appetite
For death & destruction
So deep in despair I became lost & could not find myself
My screams so deeply embedded it overshadowed my cries for
help
All I wanted was no more pain
This pain can't be numbed by OxyContin
Alone amongst many
No one really notices the one who makes everyone smile
Remembered for the moment to end up forgotten
These are what the voices in my head speak of protecting me
from
Someone tell the voices to stop
When my body drops, I'll be labeled a selfish, self-involved
sinner
All I needed was a moment
For a compassionate ear to give listen
My giving & never taking
All I want is to be love as I loved
Be wanted the way I want

I sacrificed my happiness for another's peace of mind
I say for the last time every time as if for the last time
It was my other self that handed me those bullets that loaded that
gun.
My evil reflection convinced me within its evil mind held the
cure
The solution to being a burden
The clarification to worry
The antidote to my pain
I'm no longer hidden by night; here I stand in the light of day
Alone amongst many
I put the gun to my head & pulled the trig....

THUGS OR NOMADS

There is just no way around it; no matter what community you belong to there will be a criminal element. An element in society no law abiding citizen wants to stand behind or endorse due to its corrosive nature. The criminal mentality is as old as man's existence himself; but just as man evolves so will the criminal mentality.

Let me be clear in this essay I am speaking to the non-violent offenders not rapist, murderers, and pedophiles. The criminals who would take a life unjustly, violate people sexually, or strip a child of their innocence; those criminal types have no place in society. For in those actions no humanity can be or will be found. I speak on the non-violent offenders whose population numbers clogs the American prison system.

Amerikkka and mainstream media refers to this portion of the population as "Thugs" (As do thugs themselves.) From time to time you may here "gang member," "drug dealer," any of which are used to help paint the negative picture of a person's portrayal in society. Race not withstanding usually the insinuation of racial make-up is given; never missed when the assailant(s) are either of Black or Hispanic heritages in Amerikkka. Media portrays you (thugs) as having no moral code; heathen's amongst society. But clearly when media present their expose's on the criminal lifestyle in prison they always mention criminals (thugs) living amongst each other under an unwritten moral code that is enforced by the criminals.

Brothers, Sisters, I am talking to you; those of you who identify with the labels Nigga's and Bitches; the young Black Americans who have chosen the criminal lifestyle; those who live with the label "felon." You are such a vital link to the Black Community, but your value has been disaffirmed and this potential worth not even recognized by yourselves. You are the lost warriors to a Black Nation, the wild Black American ancestral spirit of the village protectors. A resilient spirit that has evolved into street generals and soldiers, with the United States of America making you prisoners of war; the **War on Drugs** and the **War on Crime**. Making slaves out of great minds; by bringing this war down on your community they disenfranchise you from economic freedom; sentencing you to a life of serfdom. Time from your life was not enough to have paid back society for your crimes; against the people but mostly against the system. A vicious cycle designed to perpetuate, and feed off itself.

With your help in bringing upon this war you have become products of reoccurring systematical errors and injustices created by social policies, created for and used against the percentage of the population your communities (Black Americans) occupy. I say with your help because, you buy the guns and drugs from a system that outlaws them in your community; the same system that provides your community with guns and drugs. By the way, the subject of how the drugs and guns getting into the Black Community is the pink elephant in the room, one that is often mentioned but never spoke upon. Being conditioned by an unjust system has taught that we live in a Republic based on a government of Democracy with a justice system that justifies its hypocrisies. Paying the penalty for your crimes does not afford you redemption. Drug dealers in the Black American Community are the direct result of a people who have been and are being economically oppressed. The status – quo knows this and uses it to their advantage; always remember when dealing with a Devil in any situation you also deal with choices. Lack of economic opportunities will manifest itself in other ways when a civil community depends on the operation of its economics.

So many notable thugs turned gangsters have realized this and were very successful in their ventures, but could not have been without investing in their communities. By wielding their power, intelligence and strength into unification with those who held the same interest. Do the words "Super Power" sound familiar?

I say notable thugs turned gangsters because these terms imply two different types of criminal; even law enforcement recognizes this. Gangsters being higher on the food chain, even thugs themselves recognize this by using the term "O.G.," which stands for Original Gangster. Gangsters are normally Alpha's who recognize and have learned to work within the system to further their enterprise; they think in terms of wealth. Look no further than to the examples emulated by rappers and young people such as, Ellsworth, "Bumpy" Johnson, Parnell "Stacks" Edwards, The Original Freeway Rick Ross, Al "Scarface" Capone, and Charlie "Lucky" Luciano. They knew how to keep heat down and attention low and a community protected.

While thugs (also known as goons) live for the day, comfortable in the struggle, "ride or die" types, their abilities never surpass creating anything financially but rich moments. Nevertheless the primary goal/motivation for any thug or gangster is the money, financial independence. In anything you do or want to be you must increase your knowledge base. You cannot keep repeating the mistakes of those on the path before you on whatever road you choose to take.

Today's Thug must change their view on how they deal with their community; whatever your motivations are for your actions the goal has always been a clean get away. How clean is the getaway when it's your own family, friends and/or loved ones are left paying the price for your involvement in the deterioration of the Black Community? For example: children getting shot in drive-bye's, kids bringing drugs and weapons into school for protection. Everyone has somebody or something they care about or why be bothered. The proof is in the tears that even thugs cry at funerals over the bodies carried to their graves.

The Black Community you grew up in, learned to hustle in will not condone your illegal actions. But will save you a place amongst the community once you have realized the errors in your ways. The same communities (hoods) so many gangsters and thugs have claimed made them what they are. The same communities where you reminisce on happy moments back in time as a child; even though life was chaotic around you. *You owe that happiness back!*

There are some actions you can take to build your community and keep it safe without sacrificing the *"Thug Principles" you choose* to hold so dear to your hearts. But note, once again I state as long as you stay with the belief of it being okay to instill fear into the community, the community will not stand up in your defense for the breaking the law of the land. Justice concerning that system is a different fight than the one we speak on now. But the community can stand for you in the name of a righteous and just outcome. Help create a home you can come back to for a fresh start; first by you spending and investing your money in your communities; YES, that dirty non-taxable money you covet so much. The money you get from the hopeless and destitute that allows you to take care of your family than turn around and rub those spoils in your patron's faces; big cars, shiny jewels, the latest sneakers. Most of you "Thugs" are already convicted felons; *STOP SPENDING* your penitentiary chance *monies with places that do not hire non-violent drug offenders/non-violent felons. Help create more black owned businesses that will hire you* once you get out of government detention. That goes for your family members to; these corporations invest in these private and state ran penitentiaries use the prisoners for cheap labor while locked up only to deny these same men and women jobs upon release to the community. Help create banks that specialize in circulating the dollars in the Black Community that create economic opportunity; so that you may have a shot at a second shot at life if you survive your first. Buy up real estate in the Black Community to help keep the corporate oppressors from dictating your life after the hustle. At the same time, ***the Black Community cannot let pride stand in the way of these monies being used to help build a better community***. Corporate AmeriKKKa does not mind taking and using these same dollars to further their role in Black Communities economic oppression. It is simple mathematics; Beverly Hills is Beverly Hills because of the wealthy AmeriKKKan dollars which circulate a billion times over before it leaves that particular community; they invest in it to make it exclusively for them. At the same time they make it attractive to allow visitors for their dollars too, think about it. By not investing in your communities you bring political and judicial heat upon yourselves, and armed security pressure on the community.

Secondly security; keep the Black Community safe. There are many negative outside influences that affect the Black Community; none made with your well-being in mind. You are the first line of defense in any Black Community in AmeriKKKa. You are the first to be affected by any social policy, first to get the latest word on the happenings with other communities. You are the ones who know what dirt is being swept under the rugs. You come in contact with those who do what even you detest in human behavior. Pedophilia, unjust homicide, rape, elderly abuse the list can go on. Your silence, the withholding of knowledge from exposing of these horrendous people places and things that continue to happen. The same horrendous people, places and things are denying thousands of children across America from being able to live out their childhood.

The word, "Snitch" has become used so loosely that its definition has been warped. Somewhere down the line snitching has become just simply being tattled on. This ideology is flawed and bad for street business. The warped definition brings unnecessary drama and heat upon the Black Community. A snitch is a person who has profited from illegal ventures in some way shape or form and puts blame on those who has profited with him/her. The old lady across the street who saw you breaking in the house and called the cops isn't a snitch. Why wouldn't you expect anyone with a higher compassion level for humanity than you not do what they can to protect their neighbor. That is what you should expect. That is why crime was created to be an underground profession, to keep the civilians safe and out of the way. It's all in the game right? Here is something that may interest you "Snitching" also known as *"Meritorious Manumission"* was the legal act of freeing a slave for good deeds as defined by national public policy. Deeds defined as saving the white master, the invention of new medicine but mostly for "snitching" on fellow slaves. Also a tactic used in the destruction of Black unity and race loyalty. It became an informant system constantly revamped generations over to this day.

Somewhere down the line the neighbor in the hood got lost, Thugs who claimed it was all good in the hood started contributing to it not being so good. The criminals have always been there, families in the neighborhood know that, they knew/know who you were or are. Yet, these people still make small talk in store lines with you, wave and say hi as you pass each other pursuing your everyday lives. *Just as you play your position in what is refer to as the "game," you must play your position in the community* in a way your deeds may lessen its impact; soften up the lethal grip you put on the community. Although you are not fully to blame for the oppression of the Black Community as a whole, you yourselves cannot deny that you have played a negative part in how Black Communities are perceived in America. People who don't want to play your "game" should not be forced to. These steps will provide the opportunity you seek for a legal financial independence.

A message to the Thugs and Gangsters, if you don't know by now the corrupt "game" you play has been defiled. The

O'G's have relinquished control to a newer generation improperly vetted. In this newer generation you have all bosses and no soldiers. The reason for all the dissention and killings in the ranks is due to everyone believing they're leaders and no one wants to follow. The "Game" doesn't have to be a death sentence. They believe the enemy before believing those who share the same interest. This bad business causes the blind to lead the blind; if you can't take direction how are you going to lead? How do you know which map to success to use if you stop following the successful? Roads change all the time; in this game you cannot use outdated tactics (road maps) and expect to be on the road to success. Chicago's underworld scene of late as told from the Thugs and Gangster who live there is a perfect example of this; it has become every man for himself.

I'm not here to knock your hustle, judge or put you down. I'm here to uplift, enlighten and stimulate the thought process so that we as a Black Community can come closer to unification amongst ourselves. I am a felon who speaks from the experience you live. Thugs and G's wake up your self-consciousness or face being part of the reason for your own extermination.

Sources:
"Meritorious Manumission," "Black Labor White Wealth, The Search for Power & Economic Justice," by Claud Anderson, Ed. D.

"Meritorious Manumission," "Meritorious Manumission Act of 1710," By James Clingman, www.Blackpressusa.com

Subject: Education in the Black Community

"... TEACH WORKERS TO WORK AND THINKERS TO THINK; MAKE CARPENTERS OF CARPENTERS, AND PHILOSOPHERS OUT OF PHILOSOPHERS, AND FOPS OF FOOLS."

-W.E.B. Dubois 1903, "The Souls of Black Folk"

Source: The Book, "Souls of Black Folk," by W.E.B. Dubois

<u>WHERE ARE THE BODIES BURIED?</u>

White America, the Generation X's, and Millennial's
Have you ever stopped to ask where are the bodies buried?
Why not?
Are you not curious as to what part your blood line played?
For a horrific situation in which you feel blamed
There is so much you don't know
You've been purposely duped to perpetuate woes
The term "White Guilt" leaves a bad taste in your mouth
Constantly asked to fix issues over & over again
Economic oppression, police brutality, Systematical racism
White America you are in power
Have you asked grandma or grandpa?
Where are the bodies buried?
Time does dictate that if they weren't kin to the solution
Then they were participants in the problem
All in the name of your families future
Which one of your great uncles are in that famous lynching
picture?
Have you checked to see how your immigrant family benefited
from the Homestead Act?
I know you have to do research
You have to look back
At an ugly past while your new closest friends are Black
Have you asked?
Where are the bodies buried?
Or maybe you don't care
Thinking everything is just racially
All is fair

Why keep hashing up a history hard to bare?
You say lies that threaten to destroy your white privilege?
I call it the truth that opened up your eyes
No longer being able to deny your forefathers lies
Your grandfathers too
Ask them, what atrocious acts they are connected to
What did they do?
They may say, "It was a different time."
Some things will always be remembered forever in bloodlines
The sins of the father is passed down to the son
You are not to blame but the act of penance is yours to pay
I just ask you to ask
Where are the bodies buried?

WE ARE THE PROBLEM

We are the problem
Black, White & the others
Racism, Gangs, Police
Equates to guns, death & crying mothers
We don't have to love
But why let hate win?
We've created this perverted justice
Innocent is the guilty & the guilty is innocent
Mayors, Governors and Councilmen
Slashing school budgets is cutting away at our children's minds
Taking away from communities that are already deprived
Don't teach art to future artist
Because the true artist cannot be digitized
The lack of balance has the world spinning off its axis
The world took a shower & drenched itself in madness
We are the problem
Walking backwards
Picking at old wounds
As our children are carried off to the tombs
Over-seas propaganda has all of America riled up
As the instigator laughs at the 318 million people pile-up
The Euro-American predicament with the Arabs can be dated
back to the Mamelukes
Way before weapons of mass destruction
Global warming has a remedy for the world's dysfunction
If we wait long enough mother earth will kill all her children
Like she did her pet Dinosaurs
We are the problem
A call to arms without a viable plan?
How does one complain about an award that was never meant to
be for them?

Why look for recognition from those who are not recognizing?
Who needs Oscar when we can do our own enterprising?
Humanity has been corrupted by insanity
The Blackmans Kryptonite has always been his vanity
Used against him every time
Jordan's, cars, & entertainment contracts killing from the inside
Cancerous
Power has even turned old Civil Rights leaders scandalous
The numbers in the prison system tells us who society thinks the vandal is
Leaving it up to politicians to handle this
We are the problem

FLORIDA IS ONE OF NINE STATES THAT PERMANENTLY FORBID A FELON TO VOTE, EVEN AFTER THE TERM OR TIME ON PROBATION OR PAROLE HAS BEEN FULFILLED. NEITHER GEORGIA OR RHODE ISLAND GOES THAT FAR; IN BOTH STATES, A FELON CAN RECOVER THE RIGHT TO VOTE AFTER SERVING HIS TIME IN PRISON OR ON PROBATION OR PAROLE.

-Article: "2 Studies Find Laws on Felons Forbid Many Black Men to Vote,"
By Fox Butterfield
September 23, 2004

READING BETWEEN THE LINES

Stand now or fall for anything
The Devil is in the details again
As Gods debate at podiums
Standing on pedestals
Some will live
Some will die
Hell in the ground
Heaven in the Sky
Bring war to achieve peace
Become savages to conquer the beast
The winner gets to write the Bible
Christian is a Pagan disguised with a scheme
Religion is a cloak drenched in lust & greed
Sins proving to be not so deadly
Waiting on Gods judgment on pedophile priest
May HE shake the Vatican naked of secrets
To catch the demons French kissing with forked tongues
behind crumbled walls
Reverend Tax Free constantly with his hand out
The other hand, rocking the cradle, stained with blood
Ask Cain the jealous lover
Ask Mary the single mother
Sunday schools teach outdated doctrines
Why does the United States kill prophets from God?
What is the message they don't want delivered?
Maybe because they're short on their tithes
If the Devils greatest trick was proving he didn't exist
Than Gods was proving he did without ever being seen

Angels are assassins and armed guards
Does this story sound familiar
The story of Man the disgruntled son & God the absent father
Stand now or fall for anything
The Devil is in the details again

Subject: Social phrases with racist/divisive origins.

"Indian Giver"

Name that comes from the "misunderstanding" of the Native American barter-system.

"Long time no see"

Originally meant to imitate non-native English speakers.

"No can do"

Phrase used to mock Chinese immigrants who spoke Pidgin English.

"Ghetto"

Originally referred to European Districts made up of Jews or areas where Jews were confined. In new millennia a term, used to demean the poor.

"Peanut Gallery"
The name of the area where Black Americans sat in segregated venues.

"Gyp"

Derogatory term stereotyping Romani people as cheaters & thieves.
Example: "What a Gyp!"

"Call a spade a spade"

A term originated as a slur against Black Americans.

Source: ATTN.com

FUCK YOU, PAY ME!

 The American Government is a habitual offender, along with being an aider and abettor to the White Supremacist agenda against Black Americans and the Black family structure. It was written into the foundation of economic policies which helped build America from the very beginning, through slave trade and labor, implemented Acts of Law and Policy (local & Federal.) Rendering the Black American cursed to be the economic burden bearer of a capitalistic system where Blacks were once the systems top commodity. Even after slavery the countless miscarriages of justice against Black American or the countless number of United States documents that implicates the American Government in the conspiring and plotting against the Blackman and the uplifting of the Black American Family. Through the 1900's alone, J. Edgar Hoover, Director of the F.B.I. is a name that can be found on many of these directives and under-cover investigations from the 1920's till his death in the 1970's.

 The economic policies have not changed, it has only been revised, and due to the hierarchy of color and the carrying out of "The Doctrine of Unequal Exchange" in America, in 2016 Black Americans are still the life-blood of economic policy. Many of today's White American Millennials often ask, *"How do I benefit economically from slavery?"* Or, *"Why do Blacks feel they NEED reparation for slavery, why can't they earn it like my family did?"* This is a good start to understanding this economic gap between the Black and White races in America and why it exists. In the very beginning America's Economic Policies were designed for Blacks in America not to partake in the wealth of this country; to be the burden bearers of the American Dream. Black Americans have been cut-off economically at every turn in their attempts to advance economically in the United States of America. From colonial times till the end of slavery history supports how good it was/is to be White in America. What history books fail to communicate (by design) to children in public schools is exactly how good it was/is at the expense of Black Americans to be White in America. Along with how the powers of the time used strategy in national policy to make sure no claims could be made by Blacks against any White Man. Starting with the "Grandfather Clauses" protecting white slave owners and their earnings, a legal clause that kept Black Americans from taking legal action for back wages. To be followed up by the *"Black Codes"*, "The *Homestead Act"*; more currently through *"Red Lining"* and *"Predatory Lending Practices"*. All while sustaining this wealth disparity with unequal education, miseducation of the people of America, using legislation and social policy to secure a position of economic superiority. The result being a Black Community unable to protect itself, politically or socially; allowing a capitalistic system to use those financial disparities against the Black Americans as the Government profits from those disparities. Constantly feeding the disparities through the media, television and internet; feeding the people's fears and insecurities.

There are corporate businesses today in strong positions, with great wealth and power founded from slave earnings that have collected interest over the years; interest that has doubled even tripled and turned into a streaming revenue of its own. This gave White Supremacy open access to a self-generating cash flow to continue their oppressive behavior for generations to come. Some of these companies you may recognize: *Brown Brothers Harriman Co.*, invested in the capturing, transporting & trading of slaves. In 2005 *J.P. Morgan and Chase* admitted that under the name *"Citizen Bank & Canal Free Bank of Louisiana"* between 1831-1865 accepted approximately 13,000 enslaved individuals as collateral on loan and took ownership of

1,250 when plantation owners defaulted on loans. *Lehman Brothers, A.I.G., Aetna,* insured slaves for slave owners. *NY Life, Wachovia Bank* (now owned by *Wells Fargo*) accepted slaves as payment for loans. *The Rothschild & Sons Bank in London* used African slaves as collateral for loans to then *Mobile Girard Co., Central of Georgia* now *Norfolk Southern Line* valued their slaves at $31,303(est. $663,033 today). *Brooks Brothers,* slave traders turned suit retailers. All these companies have dictated the way wealth has been distributed in this country and through whose hands the wealth is distributed to. So to understand how White America of today benefits in today's time from the slavery of the past one only needs to look back at the corporate conglomerates of today and how they earned their original capitol. These corporate businesses in some way shape or form has financed the White American dream with a house, car or land by giving White Americans free land & low interest rates on loans. Corporate businesses that invested strictly in White America so that small white businesses could be opened in Black residential communities. These were corporate businesses who not too long ago in history wouldn't let a Blackman walk through the door much less sit down and give a loan with low interest to a Blackman. So if you are White in America with an ancestry line dating back in this country you will be hard-pressed to find a company that hasn't helped your blood-line any time in history.

Let's be clear, White Supremacy is a system, not a person; a system made up of Governments, Corporations and social organizations. This system has used time strategically to build its strength and endurance, but this system can be defeated; only collectively as a people not by any one individual. For the system is complex and has many moving parts. White Supremacy provides a "White Privilege" whereas whites in America can interact within the political structure and social constitutions of this country as individuals. Blacks in America do not possess this luxury. White Americans dealings with racial oppression are safe to say little to non-existent in America. Due to the security of a system created with their well-being in mind. This allows White Americans to maneuver independently through a system without a desire to act as group until White Supremacy or "White Privilege" is actively threatened.

Sun Tzu's, "Art of War" teaches that, *"If you know the enemy and know yourself, you need not to fear the result of a hundred battles."* Black America is very acquainted with their enemy, White Supremacy, but at the same time has become dependent on this enemy's capitalistic system that oppresses them. In many cases Blacks have become just as dependent on White Supremacy's opinion of them just as much as the poisons that it pumps into the Black Communities.

Black America must become economically self-sufficient in order to loosen White Supremacy's grip on its community. This will free the Black Community from its dependency on an oppressive system; no longer looking for the validation from those who wish for Black America to continue its present place in the status-quo. Once the Black Community becomes economically self-sufficient the fear of not receiving that validation will no longer hold any weight.

By first creating an industry, making a niche in the business market is essential. It will not be enough to be part of an industry that is controlled by powers that only seek to profit from the Black Community, not contributing to the building or well-being of it. Other ethnic communities whom profit from Black Communities have proven this concept as a way to preserve their own community. The Jews, Asians, Hispanics/Latinos have all done this and has White Supremacy dependent on what that community supplies instead of their consumption. According to the Bureau of Labor Statistics, November 24, 2014 Income & Spending report, Black Americans pretax income is lower than the national average. Black households' pretax income falls between $12,500 and $37,499 while each household has an expenditure of $36,149, which equals out to 79.8% of their average income before taxes. So Blacks put out more than they make on an annual basis. According to an article from Nielsen.com September 19, 2013, "African-American Consumers Are More Relevant than Ever," Blacks in America have a spending power of $1 trillion which is due to increase to $1.3 trillion by year 2017. Telecommunication companies are cleaning up in the Black Community, in the same article; 71% of the Black American population owns a smartphone compared to the U.S. population which is only 62%. Blacks have become consumption zombies meaning, as long as the Black community stays fed with the "latest trend" they stay happy, but politically silent. Like in the zombie movies when a person dies and the zombies are eating that dead persons brain, the friends are able to sneak by undetected and get away because the zombie are too into the new meal, "Consumption Zombies." White Supremacy continues to feed the Black Community the ills to maintain the financial disparities, collecting the silent black dollar.

Only Black Americans can stop this revolving door. Having no financial voice only keeps the black voice silent in the political arena, making black issues and concerns irrelevant and immaterial. The Black Community needs to have their own political party to show they have a form of unity in America; this may help control where or how the black dollar is spent in the white supremacist political structure. This is where the "Black Owned" financial institutions come in service to the Black Community. Any financial institution without stake in the community it serves means no good to those people. Your financial institution must show a strong financial presence other than mere placement of ATM machines and places of business throughout black communities. These financial institutions shall be the biggest investors in education & community youth programs that groom children in entrepreneurship. Molding independent mind states that operate strongly in business building and finance.

Yet, Black Wall Street has shown the nation the danger looming in Black communities being successful within, but without the White Supremacist system. There is a definite fear shown by the powers of the times historically seen over & over again when the Black Community becomes self-reliant and begins to come together on social & political issues. Black Lives Matter (BLM) is experiencing that today.

Is there reparation due to Black Americans? Reparations were given to the Jews from the American Government; as well as the remaining surviving Japanese Americans for their detention in WWII. Many Black Americans see this as a slap in the face from a country that knows the wrong it has done. The weight of disparity constantly put on a group of people enough to only keep them functioning as a servitude class can be seen from the beginning for Blacks in American history; from the first time they touched soil in this country up to today. Using the disparaging percentages to disgrace the Black community; using their reactions to being oppressed against them. High crime rates have a definite correlation to employment and education in any community. The high prison population amongst the Black Community is actively used to disenfranchise Black Americans. These American Corporations have set up businesses in the Black Communities only to deny Blacks employment in these communities. These are the same corporations using men and women prisoners to manufacture corporate goods to sale in a free society. The same major corporations that say these people are good enough to hire as a prison population but not as freemen & freewomen. The same corporations that can be tied back to the original human trafficking of American slave labor are the same corporations that uses today's prison labor (slave labor) and community disparages to their advantage. So is there a reparation due to Black Americans & if so, then by whom?

In closing of this essay, taking into account history and the way the facts lay out for the people. We can say America loves to hold other countries accountable monetarily or by imprisonment for atrocious acts past & present, but when it comes to being held accountable for their own terrible acts on the table of public opinion the justification is, "It happened for the greater good," leaving America above reproach with an, "It was in the name of business," attitude. In a capitalistic society, by mere design there has to be a burden class that is how economic policies are sustained under capitalism. So in America when you hear, "It was nothing personal it was only business," that's capitalism saying, unapologetically with no remorse, "Fuck You, Pay Me!"

"JESUS WAS NOT BORN IN A MANGER IN CENTRAL PENNSYLVANIA. HE WAS A MAN OF COLOR. AND THE FACT THAT WE HAVE REPRESENTED HIM FOR CENTURIES LITERALLY AS A WHITE MAN SPEAKS TO THE ENTIRE HISTORY OF WHITE SUPREMACY."

-Tim Wise

WORKING MAN

I am just a working man
Guided by morals & good character
Not politics or religion
I am the working man!
Working, cooking slowly in summer heat
4 A.M. to 7 P.M. 6 days a week
Moonlighting on the 7th to make ends meet
Society asks, "Where are the father's?"
Working their fingers to the bone
Trying to raise families
Make happy homes
Keeping smiles while the weight of the world on their domes
I Am the Working Man
Helping the next working man the best I can
He is I & I am him
No matter origin, religion or color of skin
The goal is not only to survive but to live
Take pride in a hard day's work
Paychecks calculate hours not the working man's worth
I Am the Working Man!
Who will understand?
No one looks out after the working man
But the working man
Look around observe for self
Capitol Hill relies on the working man to slave to create 1% of
its wealth
Ask no questions & be told no lies
Ask the right questions let the answers open your eyes
They call the working man a sucker
For relying on work ethic not cunning

Working man earns his keep
The working man sees fast money & never reach
Understanding dangers in moral-less money
The working man is the bee in the land of milk & honey
I Am the Working Man
Guided by morals & good character
Not politics or religion
I Am the Working Man!

KISSING THE SKY

I kissed the sky
No, I'm no junkie
No Bobby-Christina
No Skag
No Girl
Just fields green
Yep, you guessed it, it's Mary for me
The status-quo has you thinking I'm a slouch on the couch
That I am lazy, laying in doubt
Drowning in malnourished dreams
That is not the case
I am your Banker
Your Doctor
Teachers & Priest
Even the politicians in the political scene
Remind me not to smoke what they are smoking
Judges & D.A.'s in chambers choking
As they polish the chains that they intend to bind you with
For having access to the Green Ship
Extending the green hand of love for those in search of it
Now the seasons are in the middle of change
Light is being seen over the horizon
It is a new day
As I kiss the sky
Free the brothers of the green thumb
The correction to the status-quo solution
Closet smokers are now being freed
Come & indulge with me
Those with cancer or diseased come ease your pain
Pharmaceutical remedies have become an abomination
Your need outweighs my recreation

As I kiss the sky
Easing my mind
No more than the man who comes home after work & has a beer
No more than the nightly glass of wine of Ma'Dere
Only difference between the toast & the burn is the temperature
Remaining answers to questions can be found in literature.
Media speaks loud as I ride my cloud
Kissing the sky

"BY DWELLING ON THE PAST A MAN
ROBS THE PRESENT.
BUT IF MAN IGNORES THE PAST HE
ROBS THE FUTURE."

-Unknown

<u>WAKE UP</u>

Wake up!
The world is spinning off its axis
Everyone is downright tripping
As if they don't see racism still living
Black America, White America pay attention!
Wake up!
Reparations for the Jews & the Japanese
Blacks are tired of begging for justice on their knees
Repairing none of the damage done to Black America
Why no reparations because that would be a legal admittance
The proving of the White Supremacy existence
A black-eye reminder to the white race
A generation can't imagine paying for the right to white
privilege
Blacks do not speak on it & this apple pie you can taste
Black Americans are told this is all in their heads
As White Supremacy has Black America fighting over a single
slice
Justice should not be seen as a black privilege but a right
Who invented the phrase "Post-Racial?"
Since when?
Couldn't of have been invented by a Black Man
Decisions made on the Black Communities with no
representation
Local or Fed
Wake up!
We've been asleep for generations
Keeping our demon locked in the closet
Now it rears its ugly head
America has new minorities, the immigrants

The system now killing Black America dead
To replace the old burden bearers with the new
May these words run a jolt through your body
Bring you back to life
Black & White stand together & fight
You don't see the powers that be?
What they're attempting to do to you & me
Freedom is the illusion that has us thinking we're all free
WAKE UP!

1. OBJECTIVE
Example:
"I hate niggers!"
"A good nigger is a dead nigger!"

2. SUBJECTIVE
Example:
"I'm for Blacks, BUT..."
"I like Blacks, BUT..."

Source: Charles Garry, YouTube video, "Street Fighter in the Courtroom"

DEATH TO WHITE SUPREMACY

My human is a danger to your existence
I am your enemy
You eat your young in the name of greed & destruction
Attempting to play God
Selling malnourished knowledge to fuel intellect
You hide in plain sight
I know your disguise
Pulled the mask from your face to face the disgust in your eyes
Death to White Supremacy
I see the root of evil from which you feed from
The Blackman will forever be your greatest foe
Maybe that is why you try so hard to destroy Him so
Death to White Supremacy
Divided & conquered a people
500 +years & still can't kill the royal spirit
Yes, I'm the Angry Blackman
The Angry Blackman you created
Angry at how you raped beautiful Black Mothers
Angry at how you kept the father from his home
Can't forget how you've poisoned the Blackmans domes
Angry with the laws pressing on the Blackman by your thumb
For what you could not devour
You figured how to divide
Death to White Supremacy
Told me to create my own opportunity
But no dollar is of legal tender if not through you
May the spirits of Turner, Douglas, and Garvey forever haunt
you
Haunt your dreams

106

Cursing all blessings received by the blood of the Black Father
Death to you & those bourgeois traitors that watched the
slaughter
Nothing but disdain & distaste for you
And for anyone who defends you from this
Die painfully from a full thrust of the people's Right-fist
Let Knowledge, Love & Understanding be the people's legacy
Death to White Supremacy

WORD FROM THE AUTHOR

We are a nation that needs to come to grips with its own racist past & current racist attitudes and deal with the divide it has created. If by not one learning history leaves one doomed to repeat it, then this country is definitely walking backwards; regressing instead of progressing. Black America & White America are all repeating the same mistakes their forefathers made; in some ways this has made things worst.

What makes me qualified to speak on racism & social injustice you may ask. No, I am not as educated as Brothers Johnson, West, Dyson or Anderson. Nor have I ever held any office of power politically or socially. But I am everything expressed in this book, the disenfranchised, the oppressed, the branded criminal, and above all I am a Blackman in America living out a systematic racism White America expects me to accept. Growing up black in a mostly White community in a state where the Black population is less than 3% was my greatest provocation. The fighting with white kids in school for being called the word "nigger," as my so-called white friends stood in silence watching; I alone to be suspended as the other white kid was released back into school population; a situation that has become many young black males' rite of passage. Maybe it was the teachers who were in charge of shaping my mind as a child, who said I showed promise, but told me my reality was labor & servitude. I knew better, I knew even then that what I was being told was wrong. Or maybe it was the self-imposed and forced upon modern-day slavery that I've endured that gives me my Masters in oppression. Living out a life of bondage, placed into a systematical banishment where separation & punishment are used as tools and disguised as rehabilitation. And when you're banished, you're forgotten and that is when the system has its way with you. This mental and physical slavery took me on a journey from niggerdom to that of a conscientious Blackman.

Being a father, I realize my role is to be more than a man merely enjoying the process of procreation. At an early age I was moved by the spirits of great Black men like Malcolm X, Medgar Evers, Huey Newton and of course Martin Luther King Jr. Not knowing my role or place in this fight these men was fighting, but drawn to nonetheless.

I wrote this book first, to jolt the thought process. Between politicians, the media, entertainment and the internet, the ability to think for self is being taken away. We are given partial video clips and sound snippets that say what we may be thinking to keep us acting out of emotion instead of a place of rational intellect. By jolting the thought process I hope to give a fresher more up to date perspective on race in America that speaks more from the people's perspective than those in power whose agenda is to give you a perspective in order to carry out diabolical strategies.

As well as it is my goal to give a starting point, to help educate and share the knowledge I have collected along my awakening. White America's attitude towards Black America cannot be separated from the White Supremacy without counter acting the miseducation that White Supremacy has programmed into the people. In order to rebuild we must first destroy what once was, by first changing out the bricks in the foundation. Without changing the foundation the same problems will manifest themselves in other ways. I have come across many young white millennials who have no idea that black history is their history. That slavery was an economic solution continuously redesigned over generations against a group of people. U.S. History has been a lie, purposely perpetuated to keep people from realizing the evils done to give this illusion of freedom. An illusion still handed out sparingly to Black America in 2016.

Lastly but not least, to give some clarity and hopefully dispel any myths either race still carries about the other. We have a lot of scholars in this nation that speak on these same issues, all qualified and knowledgeable on these subjects. The problem becomes that even they start drowning out the voices of the people, by using complex theories and words which confuses the people and compounds the problem. Forgetting the people whom suffer is burdened by community speakers who take advantage of their situation by using the same types of language and word usage; deceit in the name of uplifting them from their oppressive situation. People in distress need to be able to understand the information clearly, so with this book I aimed to speak frankly to the people so that they may clearly understand how deep and important these issues have grown to be; and what & who the enemy is.

There are enough local & Federal studies to show crime, thuggery, and poverty are all results of collateral damage by political policy gone wrong. I urge you to study results for yourselves. In 2016, we have political candidates running for office whose voices sound nothing like those of the people; Democrat or Republican. We the people put these people from these elite clubs in charge of our government & community's well-being. Only for our trust to be violated, our belief in a free society devastated and the people even further fragmented. All while the American people still haven't sufficiently healed from the wounds of their own history. If the only reason for the popular vote (the people's vote) is to measure the people's confidence in the system then this can be used to the people's advantage. But beware less vote's will increase the fears in the political powers that be, the fear of REVOLUTION!

So may these words touch your heart as it speaks to your soul, I hope you enjoy and tell your friends about, The Reflections of Racism & Social Injustice, Mirror on the Wall.

www.ingramcontent.com/pod-product-compliance
Lightning Source LLC
Chambersburg PA
CBHW060635290526
45793CB00001B/258